Social Issues
in Literature

Race in William
Shakespeare's *Othello*

Other Books in the Social Issues in Literature Series:

Social Issues
in Literature

Race in William Shakespeare's *Othello*

Vernon Elso Johnson, Book Editor

GREENHAVEN PRESS
A part of Gale, Cengage Learning

GALE
CENGAGE Learning·

Detroit • New York • San Francisco • New Haven, Conn • Waterville, Maine • London

Elizabeth Des Chenes, *Managing Editor*

© 2012 Greenhaven Press, a part of Gale, Cengage Learning

Gale and Greenhaven Press are registered trademarks used herein under license.

For more information, contact:
Greenhaven Press
27500 Drake Rd.
Farmington Hills, MI 48331-3535
Or you can visit our Internet site at gale.cengage.com

For product information and technology assistance, contact us at

Gale Customer Support, 1-800-877-4253
For permission to use material from this text or product, submit all requests online at www.cengage.com/permissions

Further permissions questions can be emailed to permissionrequest@cengage.com

Articles in Greenhaven Press anthologies are often edited for length to meet page requirements. In addition, original titles of these works are changed to clearly present the main thesis and to explicitly indicate the author's opinion. Every effort is made to ensure that Greenhaven Press accurately reflects the original intent of the authors. Every effort has been made to trace the owners of copyrighted material.

Cover image copyright © ZEVART collection/Alamy.

LIBRARY OF CONGRESS CATALOGING-IN-PUBLICATION DATA

Race in William Shakespeare's Othello. / Vernon Elso Johnson, book editor.
    p. cm. -- (Social issues in literature)
    Includes bibliographical references and index.
    ISBN 978-0-7377-5813-9 (hardcover) -- ISBN 978-0-7377-5814-6 (pbk.)
    1. Shakespeare, William, 1564-1616. Othello. 2. Race in literature. 3. Race relations. I. Johnson, Vernon E. (Vernon Elso), 1921-
    PR3069.R33R33 2012
    822.3'3--dc23
                                                                    2011024599

Printed in the United States of America
2 3 4 5 6   16 15 14 13 12

FD222

Contents

Chapter 3: Contemporary Perspectives on Race

Introduction

While remaining highly popular for four centuries, in very different and sometimes bizarre interpretations in times of change, William Shakespeare's *Othello* has defied agreement as to its meaning, theme, delineation of character, and value. Ever since Thomas Rymer, in his book *A Short View of Tragedy* (1692), dismissed the play as a "bloody farce," critics, actors, and directors have disagreed strongly about all these factors, especially the theme of race. Charles Lamb, a nineteenth-century writer, thought the play was better read than seen. The critic A.C. Bradley considered it "the most painfully exciting" of Shakespeare's tragedies. *Othello* is unique because Shakespeare defied convention by making a black man his hero and because the action centers on a "shocking" case of miscegenation. Othello is a heroic black warrior—as well as a Christian and a Moor—who has saved Venice from the Turks and who knows little about Venetian society and even less about Venetian women. He has married a beautiful and innocent Venetian girl, Desdemona, despite her father's violent objections. Ultimately an intense jealousy, inspired by the villain Iago, drives him to passionately kill her.

To modern eyes, this is all grim tragedy, with no laughter and no comic character, but in the early seventeenth century, the first half of the play used comic devices. Iago conspires with shocking success to influence Othello until it is too late, and the play ends in violent, repugnant tragedy. Iago is also, however, a comic figure in the tradition of the stock "Vice" character of medieval morality plays, who evoked laughter from the audience. Indeed, Iago was originally played by Shakespeare's company comedian, Robert Armin. The comedic aspects of Iago can be seen in his witty exchange with Desdemona.

Over the centuries, the approach to the issue of race in the play has varied widely. Richard Burbage, Shakespeare's leading man, played Othello in blackface and made the Moor one of his great heroic roles. David Garrick in the mid-eighteenth century also played Othello in blackface with some success, though his Iago was considered better. The practice continued until the early nineteenth century, when the character's color changed. In 1814 Edmund Kean, one of the most renowned actors of the century, played Othello in light brown makeup. Thereafter, varying degrees of blackness became common. Ira Aldridge, an African American actor in the early nineteenth century, played Othello in Europe with a white Desdemona to mixed reviews. Henry Irving played Othello in bronze makeup in 1876 and then darkened the character in 1881. Sometimes, with light makeup and a judicious cutting of the script, Othello, to an observer, could have been a white desert dweller with a tan.

Then in 1943 in New York, a change occurred for America. Paul Robeson, a black man with a superb, deep voice—he was also an all-American football player and a Phi Beta Kappan in college—appeared as Othello, with Uta Hagen (a white actress) as Desdemona and José Ferrer as Iago. The production was a milestone in American theater. One of the most unusual productions occurred in the mid-twentieth century in South Africa during the last days of apartheid, when a famous white actress and an equally famous black actor used the play to make a political statement.

The articles that follow further explore the issue of race in *Othello*. Chapter 1 covers events in Shakespeare's life that impacted his writing of the play. In Chapter 2, critics deal with the basic issue of race in the play. They address, for instance, the precise color that Shakespeare intended Othello to be, the fact that Shakespeare chose to make his hero a black man, the comparative ease with which Iago undermines Othello, and the problem of a mixed-race relationship. Chapter 3 includes articles on contemporary issues of race regarding discrimination and interracial marriage.

Chronology

1453
Turks capture Constantinople.

1492
Fall of the last Moorish stronghold in Spain.

1558
Elizabeth I ascends the English throne.

War between Spain and England begins.

1564
William Shakespeare is born at Stratford-upon-Avon.

1567
In Scotland, Mary, Queen of Scots, is deposed, and eleven-month-old James VI ascends the throne of Scotland.

1568
John Shakespeare, Shakespeare's father, is elected bailiff, but rumors that he is a secret Catholic damage his standing in the community.

1576
The Theatre (the first professional theater) opens North of London.

1582
William Shakespeare marries Anne Hathaway.

1583
Shakespeare's daughter Susanna is born.

1585
Shakespeare's twins, Hamnet and Judith, are born.

1587

Mary, Queen of Scots, is executed for conspiring against Elizabeth.

1588

Another war between Spain and England begins, lasting until 1604.

c. 1588–1589

Shakespeare goes to London without his family.

His first plays are performed.

1590–1596

The Comedy of Errors, three parts of *Henry VI*, *Venus and Adonis*, *The Rape of Lucrece*, *The Taming of the Shrew*, *Two Gentlemen of Verona*, *Richard the III*, *Romeo and Juliet*, *Richard the II*, *King John*, *A Midsummer Night's Dream*, and *Love's Labours Lost* are produced.

1593

London is hit by plague, closing theaters.

1593–1594

Shakespeare acquires a share in the Lord Chamberlain's company, beginning a successful career as an investor in theaters.

1596

Shakespeare's son Hamnet dies at age eleven.

1597

The Merchant of Venice and *Henry IV, Part I*, are produced; Shakespeare invests in property in Stratford.

1598–1600

Henry IV, Part 2, *As You Like It*, *Much Ado About Nothing*, *The Merry Wives of Windsor*, *Henry V*, and *Julius Caesar* are presented.

Shakespeare's company moves to the Globe Theatre.

1600

A Moorish ambassador visits London and is entertained by Shakespeare and his company.

1601

Queen Elizabeth issues a directive that something must be done about the large numbers of black Moors that have immigrated to England due to the trouble between England and Spain.

1603

Elizabeth repeats her concern about the Moors in England.

Shakespeare's father dies after much trouble, including public suspicion that he was a secret Roman Catholic.

1602

Twelfth Night is produced.

1603

Elizabeth dies, and James Stuart (James VI of Scotland) ascends the British throne as James I.

1604

King James enters London to great fanfare. Shakespeare's company is renamed by James as the King's Men. While the company is on tour, Shakespeare finishes *Othello*.

The King's Men serve as courtiers to the Spanish Ambassador.

1605–1606

King Lear is produced, and *Macbeth* is presumably presented before James I.

1606–1611

Pericles is performed at court. *Antony and Cleopatra, Coriolanus, The Winter's Tale, The Tempest,* and *Cymbeline* are staged.

1608
Shakespeare's mother, Mary Arden, dies.

1609
Shakespeare's company purchases Blackfriars Theatre in London.

c. 1612
Shakespeare moves to Stratford-upon-Avon.

1613
Henry VIII is produced; fire destroys the Globe Theatre.

1614
The Globe reopens.

1616
Shakespeare dies.

1623
The first folio is published.

Background on
William Shakespeare

The Youth, Marriage, and Career of William Shakespeare

John F. Andrews

John F. Andrews is the author of many books and articles on Shakespeare. He founded and served as chief executive officer of the Shakespeare Guild and was editor of Shakespeare Quarterly.

William Shakespeare was born in Stratford-upon-Avon in April 1564. His father held a number of important positions in the town, but his good fortune did not last, and he failed in his attempt to secure a family coat of arms and be called a gentleman. His successful years lasted long enough, however, for him to provide his son William with a classical education. If William's youth and education were traditional, his marriage at age eighteen and his family, from whom he was separated for twenty years, were not. By 1592 he was living in London and had become an established actor and writer. He was later associated with the Lord Chamberlain's Men, a theater company. His business career flourished when he became a partner in the company. In 1604 he completed Othello, *and twelve years later he died in Stratford.*

One thing we . . . know is that if Shakespeare was a man for all time, he was also very much a man of his own age. Christened at Holy Trinity Church in Stratford-upon-Avon on 26 April 1564, he grew up as the eldest of five children reared by John Shakespeare, a tradesman who played an increasingly active role in the town's civic affairs as his business prospered, and Mary Arden Shakespeare, the daughter of a gentleman farmer from nearby Wilmcote. Whether Shake-

John F. Andrews, "William Shakespeare," *Dictionary of Literary Biography: Elizabethan Dramatists*, edited by Fredson Bowers, Detroit, MI: Gale Research Company, 1982, pp. 267–353. Copyright © 1982 by The Gale Group. All rights reserved. Reproduced by permission.

speare was born on 23 April, as tradition holds, is not known; but a birth date only a few days prior to the recorded baptism seems eminently probable, particularly in view of the fear his parents must have had that William, like two sisters who had preceded him and one who followed, might die in infancy. By the time young William was old enough to begin attending school, he had a younger brother (Gilbert, born in 1566) and a baby sister (Joan, born in 1569). As he attained his youth, he found himself with two more brothers to help look after (Richard, born in 1574, and Edmund, born in 1580), the younger of whom eventually followed his by-then-prominent eldest brother to London and the theater, where he had a brief career as an actor before his untimely death at twenty-seven.

Shakespeare's Father's Position

The house where Shakespeare spent his childhood stood adjacent to the wool shop in which his father plied a successful trade as a glover and dealer in leather goods and other commodities. Before moving to Stratford sometime prior to 1552 (when the records show that he was fined for failing to remove a dunghill from outside his house to the location where refuse was normally to be deposited), John Shakespeare had been a farmer in the neighboring village of Snitterfield. Whether he was able to read and write is uncertain. He executed official documents, not with his name, but with a cross signifying his glover's compasses. Some scholars interpret this as a "signature" that might have been considered more "authentic" than a full autograph; others have taken it to be an indication of illiteracy. But even if John Shakespeare was not one of the "learned," he was certainly a man of what a later age would call upward mobility. By marrying Mary Arden, the daughter of his father's landlord, he acquired the benefits of a better social standing and a lucrative inheritance, much of which he invested in property (he bought several houses). And by involving himself in public service, he rose by sure degrees to the highest municipal positions Stratford had to offer: chamberlain (1561), alderman (1565), and bailiff (or mayor) and justice of the peace (1568). A few years after his elevation to the office of bailiff, probably around 1576, John Shakespeare approached the College of Heralds for armorial bearings [a family crest or coat of arms] and the right to call himself a gentleman. Before his application was acted upon, however, his fortunes took a sudden turn for the worse, and it was not until 1596, when his eldest son had attained some status and renewed the petition, that a Shakespeare coat of arms was finally granted. . . .

Shakespeare's Schooling

The records we . . . have suggest that during young William's formative years he enjoyed the advantages that would have accrued to him as the son of one of the most influential citizens of a bustling market town in the fertile Midlands. When he was taken to services at Holy Trinity Church, he would have sat with his family in the front pew, in accordance with his father's civic rank. There he would have heard and felt the words and rhythms of the Bible, the sonorous phrases of the 1559 Book of Common Prayer [the Church of England's service book], the exhortations of the Homilies [sermons]. In all likelihood, after spending a year or two at a "petty school" to learn the rudiments of reading and writing, he would have proceeded, at the age of seven, to "grammar school." Given his father's social position, young William would have been eligible to attend the King's New School, located above the Guild Hall. . . .

During his many long school days there, young Shakespeare would have become thoroughly grounded in Latin, acquired some background in Greek, and developed enough linguistic facility to pick up whatever he may have wanted later from such modern languages as Italian and French. . . . If Shakespeare's references to schooling and schoolmasters in the plays are a reliable index of how he viewed his own years as a student, we must conclude that the experience was more tedious than pleasurable. But it is difficult to imagine a more suitable mode of instruction for the formation of a Renaissance poet's intellectual and artistic sensibility. . . .

Shakespeare's Unconventional Marriage and Family

Once his school years ended, Shakespeare married, at eighteen, a woman who was eight years his senior. We know that Anne Hathaway was pregnant when the marriage license was issued by the Bishop of Worcester on 27 November 1582, because a daughter, Susanna, was baptized in Holy Trinity six months later on 26 May 1583. We have good reason to believe that the marriage was hastily arranged: there was only one reading [instead of three] of the banns (a church announcement preceding a wedding that allowed time for any legal impediments against it to be brought forward before the ceremony took place), an indication of unusual haste. But whether the marriage was in any way "forced" is impossible to determine. . . .

What we do have to go on is certainly compatible with the suspicion that William and Anne were somewhat less than ardent lovers. They had only two more children—the twins, Hamnet and Judith, baptized on 2 February 1585—and they lived more than a hundred miles apart, so far as we can tell, for the better part of the twenty-year period during which Shakespeare was employed in the London theater. . . .

But even if there is reason to speculate that Shakespeare may not have always been faithful to the marriage bed, there is much to suggest that he remained attached to Anne as a husband. In 1597 he purchased one of the most imposing houses in Stratford—New Place, across the street from the Guild Chapel—presumably settling his wife and children there as soon as the title to the property was clear. He himself retired to that Stratford home, so far as we can determine, sometime between 1611 and 1613. And of course he remembered Anne in his will, bequeathing her the notorious "second-best bed"—which most modern biographers regard as a generous afterthought (since a third of his estate would have gone to the wife by law even if her name never occurred in the document) rather than the slight that earlier interpreters had read into the phrasing.

Naturally we would like to know more about what Shakespeare was like as a husband and family man. But most of us would give just as much to know what took place in his life between 1585 (when the parish register shows him to have become the father of twins) and 1592 (when we find the earliest surviving reference to him as a rising star in the London theater). . . . All we can say for certain is that by the time his children were making their own way to school in rural Stratford, William Shakespeare had become an actor and writer in what was already the largest city in Europe.

Shakespeare's Early Theatrical Career

Shakespeare probably traveled the hundred miles to London by way of the spires of Oxford, as do most visitors returning from Stratford to London today. But why he went, or when, history does not tell us. It has been plausibly suggested that he joined an acting troupe (the Queen's Men) that was one player short when it toured Stratford in 1587. If so, he may have migrated by way of one or two intermediary companies to a position with the troupe that became the Lord Chamberlain's Men in 1594. The only thing we can assert with any assurance is that by 1592 Shakespeare had established himself as an actor and had written at least three plays. . . .

One gathers . . . , that, like other playwrights of the period, Shakespeare was careful not to refer too overtly to deficiencies in the well-to-do members of his audiences, especially when such members might include the nobility or persons close to them. After all, an acting company's livelihood depended upon its securing and retaining favor at Court—not only because of the extra income and prestige that accrued from periodic Court performances commissioned by the Master of the Revels, but even more fundamentally because a company could perform in or near London only if it were licensed to do so by the Crown and enjoyed the protection of a noble or royal patron. A prudent playwright would not wish to jeopardize his company's standing with the monarch. And Shakespeare and his colleagues—the other "sharers" who owned stock in the company that was known as the Lord Chamberlain's Men from 1594 until 1603 (when Queen Elizabeth died and was succeeded by King James I) and the King's Men thereafter (having received a patent as the new monarch's own players)—must have been prudent, because theirs was by far the most prosperous and the most frequently "preferred" theatrical organization in the land, from its inception in the early 1590s until the triumph of Puritanism finally brought about the closing of the theaters half a century later in 1642.

Shakespeare as a Businessman

Shakespeare's position with the Lord Chamberlain's Men was a source of professional stability that probably had a great deal to do with his growth and maturation as a writer. For one thing, it freed him from some of the uncertainties and frustrations that must have been the lot of other playwrights, virtually all of whom operated as free-lancers selling their wares to impresarios such as Philip Henslowe (often for as little as five pounds), and most of whom thus forfeited any real say about how their plays were to be produced and, in time (if a given acting company so wished or if chance provided), published. From at least 1594 on Shakespeare was a stockholder of the theatrical organization for which he wrote his plays. After 1598 (when the sons of the recently deceased James Burbage, Cuthbert and Richard, invited four of the

Mr. WILLIAM

SHAKESPEARES

COMEDIES,
HISTORIES, &
TRAGEDIES.

Publifhed according to the True Originall Copies.

Frontispiece to the first quarto edition of the collected works of William Shakespeare, engraved by Martin Droeshout circa 1623. © Rischgitz/Getty Images.

principal actors in the Lord Chamberlain's Men to become their partners and put up half the capital needed to rebuild the Theatre across the Thames as the Globe), Shakespeare was also a co-owner of the playhouse in which that company performed the plays. As such, he shared in all the profits the Lord Chamberlain's Men took in at the gate, and he was undoubtedly a participant in most, if not all, of the major decisions affecting the company's welfare. We know from the surviving legal records of the playwright's various business transactions that he prospered financially by this arrangement: like his father, Shakespeare invested wisely in real estate, purchasing properties in both Stratford and London. And we can infer from the evidence of his rapidly developing sophistication as a dramatist that Shakespeare's membership in a close-knit group of theatrical entrepreneurs also helped him flourish artistically. . . .

Othello and Shakespeare's Other Revenge Plays

After *Measure for Measure* [a tragicomedy], so far as we can tell, Shakespeare turned his attention entirely to tragedy for three or four years. By 1604, apparently, he completed *Othello*, the second of the four major tragedies. By 1605 he seems to have completed *King Lear*, the third and, in the estimation of many, the greatest of the tragedies. And by 1606 he had evidently written the last of the "big four," *Macbeth*. During the next two to three years Shakespeare turned once more to classical sources, completing *Antony and Cleopatra* and *Coriolanus*, respectively, in 1606–1607 and 1607–1608, and abandoning *Timon of Athens* (if we are correct in thinking that it was left unfinished and unacted) sometime around 1607 or 1608. Only two of these plays appeared in quarto printings, *King Lear* in 1608 in what many scholars now regard as a memorial reconstruction of an early version of the play, and *Othello* in 1622 in a text of uncertain provenance. Most modern editions of *King Lear* and *Othello* follow the First Folio texts as their prime authorities, supplementing those texts where appropriate with readings or passages from the quartos (although, particularly with *King Lear*, where the two printings of the play are thought by some to derive from discrete and self-consistent earlier and later scripts of the play, there is now a school of thought that opposes conflating the Folio and quarto versions). The other three tragedies all appeared for the first time in the 1623 Folio.

When we come to *Othello* fresh from a reading of either *Hamlet* or *Measure for Measure*, we can see links with the earlier plays in *Othello*'s treatment of sexual love and in the play's preoccupation with ethical questions that turn, ultimately, on revenge versus forgiveness. For whatever else *Othello* is, it is a species of revenge tragedy. To the extent that Iago is impelled by something more specific than what [nineteenth-century English poet Samuel Taylor] Coleridge termed "motiveless malignity," he is motivated by a determination to prove Othello "egregiously an ass" for promoting Michael Cassio rather than Iago to the lieutenancy. And Iago's vengeance extends to Cassio as well as to Othello. But more to the point, once Iago convinces Othello that Desdemona has slept with Cassio, he transforms Othello into the principal tool as well as the prime object of his revenge.

Othello as "Great of Heart"

Iago's "poison" is administered in two doses. First he provides enough circumstantial "proof" to make plausible his insinuation that Desdemona has been unfaithful to Othello. But second and far more crucial, he works Othello into such a frenzy that he is unable to give serious consideration to any response to his "knowledge" other than revenge. Once Othello becomes persuaded that Desdemona is indeed guilty of infidelity, his instinctive reaction is to exclaim "But yet the pity of it, Iago! O Iago, the pity of it, Iago!" To which Iago replies "If you are so fond over her iniquity, give her patent to offend, for if it touch not you, it comes near nobody." Here as elsewhere Iago's method is to get Othello to focus, not on Desdemona, but on himself. By constantly reiterating such terms as "reputation," "good name," and "honor," Iago plays upon Othello's insecurity as a Moorish alien and implies that his wife's behavior will make him the laughingstock of Venetian society.

It is a mark of his worthiness as a tragic hero that, to the end, Othello retains the "free and open nature" that made him vulnerable to Iago in the beginning, Iago may manipulate Othello into committing a rash and terrible murder, but he cannot reduce Othello entirely to a blunt instrument of the ensign's vengeance. Before Othello can bring himself to suffocate Desdemona, he must first delude himself into believing that he is an agent of divine justice. And even in that role his innate compassion leads him to offer his wife a moment to prepare her soul for heaven. It is true that Othello becomes angry again when Desdemona fails to confess to a crime that would have been inconceivable to her, but one of the things that makes his act pathetic rather than malicious is the fact that he continues to express his devotion for Desdemona even as he forces himself to snuff out her life. In that sense as well as in Iago's more cynical sense, then, Othello becomes "an honorable murderer." And no matter how we judge Othello's final speech and "bloody period," we have to agree with Cassio's assessment that "he was great of heart." . . .

Shakespeare's Death and Cultural Immortality

Tradition holds that Shakespeare returned to Stratford for his declining years, and three years after the burning of the Globe his own flame went out. Following his death on 23 April 1616, he was laid to rest where fifty-two years earlier he had been christened. Shortly thereafter, a monument to his memory was erected above the tomb in Holy Trinity, and that monument is still in place for Shakespeare admirers to see today. But an even greater monument to his memory appeared seven years later, when his theatrical colleagues, John Heminge and Henry Condell (both of whom had been mentioned in the playwright's will) assembled a large volume of his collected plays. The 1623 First Folio was a labor of love, compiled as "an office to the dead, to procure his orphans guardians" and "to keep the memory of so worthy a friend and fellow alive as was our Shakespeare."

Our Shakespeare. It is not without exaggeration that the book that preserves what is probably his most reliable portrait and the most authoritative versions of the majority of his dramatic texts (indeed the *only* surviving versions of half of them) has been called "incomparably the most important work in the English language." In the words and actions that fill his poems and plays, in the performances that enrich our theaters and silver screens, in the countless off-shoots to be found in other works of art, and in the influence the playwright continues to have on virtually every aspect of popular culture throughout the world, now as much as in the age of Elizabeth and James, Shakespeare lives.

Historical Events Influenced Shakespeare's Writing of *Othello*

Peter Ackroyd

Peter Ackroyd, a prolific and eminent English biographer and novelist, is the chief book reviewer for the Times *of London.*

William Shakespeare likely composed Othello *in the summer of 1604, just after the triumphal parade marking the beginning of King James I's reign over England and while other members of his company, now called the King's Men, were on tour.* Othello *opened at the Globe Theatre the following fall. The play is gloomy in keeping with the death of Queen Elizabeth I and the death and suffering caused by the plague, which kept most theaters closed until April 1604. In the background of the play is Spain's continuing battle to expel the Moors (descendants of Muslim conquerors from North Africa) from the country. Thus* Othello *is a Moor, and the chief villain, Iago, has a Spanish name. Also in the background is the visit to England years earlier of the Moorish ambassador and the rumor that the Spanish king, Philip II, had strangled his wife out of insane jealousy.* Othello *is the only play of Shakespeare's with a contemporary setting. He took the basics of his plot from a prose tale by Giraldi Cinthio.*

The King's Men were travelling in the spring and summer of 1604; they visited Oxford, for example, in May and June. It is unlikely . . . that Shakespeare now travelled with them. During this period he completed two plays that were performed at court towards the close of 1604; *Othello* and

Peter Ackroyd, "I Will a Round Unvarnished Tale Deliver," *Shakespeare: The Biography*, New York, NY: Random House, Inc., 2005, pp. 425–632. Copyright © 2005 by Random House, Inc. All rights reserved. Reproduced by permission.

Measure for Measure were staged respectively in November and December of this year. Since the public theatres had been allowed to open again in April, one or both of these plays had first been shown at the Globe. . . . It has been suggested that *Othello* and *Measure for Measure* are both dark plays for a dark time, born of the plague and the queen's death, with the tragedy of Othello and Desdemona preceding the bitter and forlorn story of Angelo and Isabella [in *Measure for Measure*]. But in fact they seem to have been written in a period of general rejoicing at the new king's accession, with Shakespeare reaching the pinnacle of his social eminence.

Battle Between Spain and the Moors

The King's Men were acting as courtiers for the Ambassador Extraordinary of Spain in the period when Othello "the Moor" was being created. The "Moor" himself is of Spanish origin while two of the other characters in the play, Roderigo and Iago, have recognisably Spanish names. Even in the period when Shakespeare was writing there was a concerted Spanish effort to expel the very large population of Moors from their country. The Moors, like the Jews, were the victims of European racial prejudice. There was also a large colony of Moors in London, refugees from Spanish persecution. Elizabeth I issued an edict against "the great number of negars and blackamoors which are crept into the realm since the troubles between Her Highness and the King of Spain."

In 1600 a Moorish ambassador for the King of Barbary came to Elizabeth's court, and became an object of fascinated attention. There is ample reason for Shakespeare to have seen, and even spoken with, him. He played before him at court, during the Christmas season. The Moor sat for his portrait during this visit, too, and the image of this dignified if somewhat withdrawn figure must have impressed itself upon Shakespeare's conception of Othello. At the age of forty-two he looks haunted, forever watchful. It is a mistake to consider

Othello to be of African or West Indian origin, as is often the case in modern productions. He was of Moorish stock, olive-skinned, and Shakespeare portrays him as "black" for the purposes of theatrical emphasis and symbolism. In Shylock [the villain in *The Merchant of Venice*] Shakespeare had created a character of some complexity; by the time he came upon Othello, he had become even more interested in the role and nature of the scapegoat. But it would be a mistake to assume that he had any overt humanitarian purpose. Instead he had a keen eye and ear for theatrical intrigue.

Rumors that King Philip Had Strangled His Wife

There are other contemporary matters that must be seen in the context of *Othello*, if only because they would have been known to every member of the audience who witnessed the first production. King James had a pronounced sympathy for the Spanish state; that is why Shakespeare and his fellows were entertaining the Ambassador Extraordinary in Somerset House. But there was also a well-attested story publicised throughout Europe that the previous king of Spain, Philip II, was an insanely jealous husband who had strangled his wife in her bed. What is more, he had become suspicious of her when she had inadvertently dropped her handkerchief. These parallels are too close to be coincidental. The fact that Cyprus becomes the scene of the tragic action of *Othello* is also explicable in these terms. Cyprus was once a Venetian protectorate but had been occupied by Turkish forces for more than thirty years, and thus posed a threat to Spanish as well as Venetian interests in the region. King James himself had written a poem upon the subject. So Shakespeare was deliberately reflecting the interests and preoccupations of the sovereign. During the present reign of Philip III, too, Spain was at odds with the republic of Venice. . . .

Othello and Current Events

It is undoubtedly true that Shakespeare's imagination, magnetised, as it were, around Spain, had drawn in everything. He had become, for the purposes of this play, a vessel for all things Spanish.

So it would be wrong to state that Shakespeare never wrote a play concerning contemporary life. *Othello* was a very modern drama, refracting all the circumstances of the period. Shakespeare also read some recently published translations that suited his purpose—among them [Moorish writer John Leo's] *A Geographical Historie of Africa* and [Roman writer] Pliny's *Historie of the World*. He also read Sir Lewis Lewkenor's *The Commonwealth and Government of Venice*. These books were published in 1600, 1601 and 1599 respectively, so we may plausibly imagine Shakespeare as a haunter of bookstalls, picking up any recently printed volumes as a spur to his creativity. . . .

Shakespeare's Learning

The question of Shakespeare's learning has vexed many commentators. Its extent can perhaps be measured in the simple statement that he learned as much as he needed to learn. . . .

It is possible that he could read both French and Italian, but he preferred to use translations wherever possible. It is not a question of laziness but of efficiency. . . .

He may have owned a library or carried his store of books with him in a book-chest. He mentions libraries only twice in his published work. Yet he could have used the libraries of patrons, such as [the Earls of] Southampton or Pembroke, and of course he might have lingered and read in [childhood friend and publisher] Richard Field's bookshop. He must have had one or two books physically close to him, however, since there are occasions when he quotes long passage almost verbatim from [Greek historian and biographer] Plutarch and from [contemporary English chronicler Raphael] Holinshed. . . .

Shakespeare's Primary Source for *Othello*

When he read his primary source narrative for *Othello*, Giraldi Cinthio's *Hecatommithi*, he must have been struck—inspired, rather—by its first sentence. "*Fu gia in Venezia un Moro.*" There was a Moor in Venice. Venice had been the site of his first outcast, in the person of Shylock. Othello was another example of the dispersed and dispossessed, the wanderers of the earth. There was a Moor in Venice. Cinthio's narrative is a prose tale, but something within it stirred all the powers of Shakespeare's sympathetic imagination. He immensely deepened and broadened the story, so that the first two acts of the play in particular bear very little resemblance to any possible originals. A measure of his contribution is to be found in the fact that all the names of the characters, apart from that of Desdemona, were formulated by him. He also revised his play, giving Desdemona more pathos and credibility, and, because he must have realised in performance that Emilia, the wife of Iago, had become too unsympathetic a creation, he gave her more dialogue with Desdemona so that she gained in sympathy.

Performance of *Othello*

The play, with the title of *The Moor of Venis* by "Shaxberd," was performed for the king and his court on 1 November 1604 in the Banqueting House at Whitehall. It was not written for private performance, of course, and it had already been played at the Globe and in the guildhalls of the company's provincial tours. Richard Burbage, as Othello, would have "blacked up." There was no occasion for subtlety in the presentation. A versifier later commented upon Burbage's role as "the grieved Moor." One curiosity concerns the part of Othello. When [contemporary author and actor] Ben Jonson described Shakespeare's own character he considered that he "was (indeed) honest, and of an open, and free nature." He is quoting almost verbatim from Iago's description of Othello:

The Moore is of a free and open nature,

That thinkes men honest, that but seeme to be so.

It may be an inadvertent recollection on Jonson's part, but does it suggest that Shakespeare was in some sense "like" Othello? The theme of sexual jealousy runs deeply through many of Shakespeare's plays. Could Jonson have known that Shakespeare harboured suspicions about his wife in Stratford? . . .

If a boy played Desdemona, he must have been a skilful and remarkable actor. He had to suggest a certain eroticism within Desdemona's innocence; as the German philosopher Heinrich Heine put it, "What repels me most every time are Othello's references to his wife's moist palm." The boy actor would also have had a good voice, able to sing popular ballads. Since Desdemona's willow song is absent from the first published version of the play, however, it is likely that for some performances he was unavailable for the part.

It might come as a surprise to contemporary audiences that Iago, customarily seen as the epitome of evil in modern productions, was initially played by the company's resident clown and fool, Robert Armin. Iago was in the comic mode, and spoke to the audience in his confidential soliloquies. Charles Gildon, at the end of the seventeenth century, disclosed that

> I'm assur'd from very good hands, that the Person that Acted Iago was in much esteem for a Comoedian, which made Shakespeare put several words, and expressions into his part (perhaps not so agreeable to his Character) to make the Audience laugh, who had not yet learnt to endure to be serious a whole Play.

Iago's role as comedian also fits the essentially comic structure of the play itself. Of course Gildon is alluding here to the sexual bawdry and innuendo in which Iago indulges with Desdemona, but he is being less than fair to Shakespeare. The dramatist loved sexual slang, and would not have considered it as writing "down" to any audience. It was a part of his imagination. As for being "serious" for "a whole Play" there is not one drama of Shakespeare's which aspires to that unity of mood or tone. Comedy and tragedy were equal parts of his art.

Othello, the King's Men, and James I

Anthony Holden

Anthony Holden, an English writer and commentator, has written biographies of William Shakespeare, Princess Diana, Sir Laurence Olivier, and Prince Charles, among others.

In 1603, the year before Shakespeare finished Othello, *James VI of Scotland became James I of England after the death of Elizabeth I. It began the period of Shakespeare's greatest acclaim. A few days after James's spectacular entry into London, he chose Shakespeare's company to be placed under royal patronage, renaming it the King's Men. This, of course, placed all the members of the company, including Shakespeare in a position of privilege. For one thing, it meant that when audiences fled the city and most theaters were closed because of the plague that year, the King's Men still had work performing for the king, his courtiers, and foreign visitors. Still, it was a period of spiritual trouble for the aging Shakespeare, and the result in the fall of 1604 was the dark play* Othello, *whose villain's name, Iago, is Spanish for "James."*

Not until she was on her deathbed did Elizabeth finally deign to name her heir, whispering to attendant Privy Councillors that she could not possibly be succeeded by anyone but a king—'and who should that be but our cousin of Scotland?' Horsemen rushed the news to Edinburgh, whence King James VI of Scotland and I of England embarked on a triumphal progress south. . . .

Anthony Holden, "The King's Man," *William Shakespeare: His Life and Work*, New York, NY: Little, Brown and Company, 1999, pp. 205–238. Copyright © 1999 by Little, Brown and Company. All rights reserved. Reproduced by permission.

The King's Men

Within ten days of arriving in London, although besieged by other claims for his attention, the new King took the Lord Chamberlain's troupe under his own royal patronage. Shakespeare was now one of the King's Men. . . .

By taking them under his royal wing, James had officially confirmed the standing of the Lord Chamberlain's Men as the leading theatrical company in the land. The royal patronage bestowed on London's other main companies was distinctly less grand, the Admiral's troupe and the Earl of Worcester's becoming merely Prince Henry's and Queen Anne's Men. As one of the King's Men, Shakespeare was now an ex-officio Groom of the Bedchamber, a member of the royal household entitled to four and a half yards of scarlet cloth for his livery, to be worn at the coronation. . . .

Shakespeare's Popularity

James was to prove a valuable patron to Shakespeare and his fellows. In the thirteen years between the King's accession and the poet's death, the King's Men would play at court no fewer than 187 times—an average of thirteen royal command performances a year, compared with three during Elizabeth's reign. [James] paid twice as much, what's more, reckoning his post-prandial [after-dinner] entertainment a legitimate drain on the Privy Purse [the king's private income]. For the King's Men, this meant gainful employment even when the theatres were closed by the plague—as, for instance, that August, when they were paid £21 12s [shillings] to entertain the new Spanish ambassador, Don Juan Fernandez de Velasco, at Somerset House (which, with a peace treaty with England's old foe in the offing, the King had placed at his disposal).

As the upper crust evacuated London for the duration, which turned out to be almost a year, the King repaired to Wilton House, near Salisbury, as a guest of the Countess of Pembroke. In the autumn of 1603 his players were summoned to perform *As You Like It* there, for which they were paid the munificent sum of £30. 'We have the man Shakespeare with us,' the Countess wrote to her son William, who had his own troupe of players, the Earl of Pembroke's Men. . . .

Shakespeare's Comedies Come to an End

In the year from November 1604 to 31 October 1605, according to the accounts of the Master of the Revels, Shakespeare and the King's Men performed at court at least eleven times—ten different plays, including seven by Shakespeare, mostly hardy annuals from *The Comedy of Errors* and *Love's Labour's Lost* to *The Merry Wives of Windsor*. The one play James specifically asked to see twice was *The Merchant of Venice*. In *Measure for Measure*, Shakespeare was again taking risks: gratifying the King's interest in justice and mercy while chronicling his own disenchantment with both.

As a comedy, his twelfth, it seems to end a line of dramatic inquiry he had been pursuing throughout the fifteen or so years of his writing career, refining it to the point where the twentieth century has trouble calling this a comedy, preferring to label it a 'problem' play. Its bleak mood, savage humour and 'predominant harshness of tone'—a comedy which takes place almost entirely in darkness, shadows or dingy interiors—suggests Shakespeare felt he had mined this vein to its very core, to what he considered a natural conclusion. The problems posed by the final scene further suggest that, immersed in Cinthio, he was already brooding about *Othello*.

Measure for Measure was the last comedy Shakespeare would write. The great tragedies immediately ahead were already taking shape in his mind. . . .

Personal Problems and a Dart Play

If Shakespeare was developing problems, they were more spiritual than physical. As he turned forty, the world was too much with him. The exuberant gaiety of his early work is no more.

His last plays to be called comedies are the work of a gravely reflective man, nostalgic for times past, not so much cynical as sceptical, more battle-hardened than world-weary, old before his time.

Forty was quite an age for the day, five years beyond the average life expectancy, especially for those choosing the lawless, polluted, disease-ridden life of the capital. Where his soul had been scarred by the death of his son, the demise of his father had merely aged him. The natural *joie de vivre* [joy of living] had gone, to return only fitfully in his writings, replaced by the more sombre, searching spirit of inquiry which would now produce his mature masterworks.

The Theme of Sexual Jealousy in *Othello*

Whatever else was troubling him, Shakespeare next chose to address a subject unexplored in any of his previous twenty-six plays, but to which he would return, as if obsessively: sexual jealousy. Whether reading or watching *Othello* and *The Winter's Tale*, or indeed lingering over the Sonnets, it is hard to resist the conclusion that the poet capable of evoking the 'green-eyed monster' in such violent language must have experienced its unique horrors himself.

Othello and Desdemona make 'the beast with two backs'; her father, Brabantio, is told that an 'old black ram' is 'tupping your white ewe'; Leontes thinks he sees his wife and best friend 'paddling palms and pinching fingers', then turns to tell the audience:

There have been,

Or I am much deceiv'd, cuckolds ere now,

And many a man there is, even at this present,

Now, while I speak this, holds his wife by th' arm,

That little thinks she has been sluiced in 's absence,

And his pond fished by his next neighbour, by

Sir Smile, his neighbour.

It is impossible to believe that the man who wrote these lines, who fastened on that word 'sluiced' and the image of 'Sir Smile, his neighbour', had not himself experienced the full anguish of sexual jealousy. . . . But who might have caused him such powerful emotions at this particular time, feeding the frenzy behind Othello's 'goats and monkeys'? . . .

The Moorish Ambassador and Africa

These are passing thoughts, no more, for Shakespeare himself surely knew enough of the pangs of jealousy. . . . The later Sonnets are full of the agonies which would now shudder so terribly through *Othello*. He had also been a player at court four years earlier during a prolonged visit by the Moorish ambassador of the King of Barbary, an exotic figure who attracted much attention; he and his Muslim retinue, being 'strange in their ways', were naturally described as 'Barbarians'. A portrait of the ambassador painted during his visit . . . settles the age-old debate about the precise ethnic background Shakespeare intended to convey by the word Moor. 'Is it too fanciful,' asks one of the play's most recent (and perceptive) editors, 'to suppose that this very face haunted Shakespeare's imagination and inspired the writing of his tragedy?'

'No nation in the world is so subject unto jealousy, for they will rather lose their lives than put up any disgrace in the behalf of their women,' wrote John Leo, a Barbary-bred Moor, of his 'very proud and high-minded, and wonderfully addicted unto wrath' fellow-countrymen. 'Their wits are but mean, and they are so credulous that they will believe matters impossible which are told them.' Shakespeare undoubtedly consulted John Pory's English translation of Leo's *A Geographical History of Africa*, published in 1600 during the Moorish embassy to London. Leo himself speaks of women who wear gowns 'curiously

Depiction of Shakespeare in his study. © Hulton Archive/Getty Images.

embroidered', just like that fateful handkerchief. Pory's summary of Leo's 'great travels' mirrors Othello's vivid account of his own adventures, as does Philemon Holland's 1601 translation of Pliny's *Natural History of the World*, which mentions 'the medicinal gum of the Arabian trees, mines of sulphur, a state made of chrysolite [a semiprecious stone], mandragora and coloquintida [poisonous herbs]', not to mention the Pontic Sea, the Anthropophagi [cannibals], and 'men whose heads / Do grow beneath their shoulders'.

Relevance of Venice, Spain, and Africa

For the power structure of Venice—then renowned in England for the loose morals of its courtesans—Shakespeare consulted Sir Lewis Lewkenor's *The Commonwealth and Government of Venice*, largely a translation of the Latin text of Cardinal Contrarini, published in 1599. But his main source was again Cinthio, specifically a short story from his collection entitled *Hecatommithi*, published in Italy in 1565. We do not know of an English translation available to Shakespeare, though versions existed in French and Spanish. Again, he makes countless significant advances on the original story; to judge how far he rose above his source this time, we need only note that Cinthio's Iago teamed up with Othello to kill Desdemona, beating her to death with a stocking filled with sand, then pulling down the ceiling in an attempt to make her murder look like an accident.

Again, Cinthio appears to have based his own tale on a true recent episode. In 1565 the story circulated Europe of an Italian diplomat in France drawn home by false reports, spread by his enemies, of his wife's infidelity; having confronted her with the accusations, he accepted her denials, but strangled her anyway—apologising as he did so—in the name of his honour. Shakespeare plays with time, with class, nobility, credulity, domesticity, with the concepts of knowledge and honesty. In Othello he creates the first example of a 'noble' black man, however fallible, in Western literature. At a time when [the queen's chief adviser William] Cecil was hearing protests about the number of blackamoors 'infiltrating' English society, it was (to say the least) bold of Shakespeare to make a noble non-savage the most sympathetic of all his tragic heroes—as enlightened on racial prejudice, as pioneeringly anti-bigotry, as he had been in *The Merchant of Venice.*

The Most Time-Bound Tragedy

In Iago he fashions the most diabolical of all his images of evil incarnate, made all the more chilling for the fact that . . . he does not kill anyone—except by proxy. The ensign's supposed motives for poisoning his master's mind against his bride—that he had been passed over for the lieutenantship, that Othello had seduced his own wife—are so inadequate (the latter stretching even his own belief) as to take on the eeriest notes of bewildered, almost apologetic self-justification. [Nineteenth-century English poet Samuel Taylor] Coleridge's famous verdict, 'the motive-hunting of motiveless malignity', has never been bettered.

In the absence of any supernatural element (as in *Hamlet* and *Macbeth*), or extreme psychological disturbance (as in *Lear*), *Othello* remains the most intimate, the most direct of Shakespeare's four great tragedies. It is as a private, not as a public man that its protagonist is undone, causing passing political embarrassment to the state to which he has done some service, but no great disruption of the natural order. This play is more 'insistently time-bound' than the others . . .

Was the King offended by *Othello* when it was performed before him on 1 November 1604? We have no reason to suppose so. But that Machiavellian villain's name, of course, means James—in Spanish, moreover, the language of England's old enemy, while the names of all the play's other Venetians are appropriately Italian. Refusing to believe that Shakespeare could be so 'tactless', some scholars have used this reason to look for others to move the play earlier, to make it an Elizabethan rather than a Jacobean work—coming straight after *Hamlet*, before the old Queen's death, before peace was made with Spain.

Social Issues in Literature

CHAPTER 2

Othello and Race

The Question of Othello's Color

Norman Sanders

Norman Sanders taught at the University of Illinois and was the Lindsay Young Professor of Humanities at the University of Tennessee. He is the author and editor of many books on William Shakespeare.

Sources that provided the Elizabethan public with information about Africans contributed to the general suspicion that people of the black race were going to creep into England and "pollute" the population. Evidence of this can be found in Queen Elizabeth I's stated fear of Africans in England. Exactly what color Othello is supposed to be has long been a matter of controversy, causing customs and makeup to vary from performance to performance. Many lines in Othello *suggest that it is not just a tawny skin that makes Venetians regard his appearance as unnatural in that white community. Reference is made to Othello's thick lips and, repeatedly, to his blackness. But Shakespeare sometimes used the word* black *to refer to brunettes and Arabs, and the widely publicized appearance in England in 1600 of a group of Arabs may have influenced his creation of Othello. According to Sanders, there is just no way of being absolutely sure about what color or race Shakespeare intended Othello to be.*

The dramatic emphasis placed on the racial difference between Othello and the other characters in the play is one of Shakespeare's most striking departures from [Giraldo] Cinthio's tale [on which it is based]. . . . Yet despite the theme's obvious centrality in the play, there is no agreement about which race exactly it was that Shakespeare had in mind for Othello. . . .

Norman Sanders, "Introduction," *Othello*, edited by Norman Sanders, New York, NY: Cambridge University Press, 2003, pp. 1–51. Copyright © 2003 by Cambridge University Press. All rights reserved. Reproduced by permission.

It is noticeable that it is no part of even Iago's huge racial antagonism to Othello that his commanding officer is not a Venetian; and Brabantio, before the play begins, viewed the Moor only as a distinguished soldier and honoured guest. It is only when race is connected with miscegenation [marriage between different racial groups] that it becomes a highly-charged emotional issue for the internationally-minded Venetians; and it was probably more so for the insular theatregoers of Jacobean England.

Sources on Africans

The origins of popular English knowledge of Africa and its inhabitants may be traced to *Mandeville's Travels*, which discussed such topics as racial characteristics and geographical locations of the varying degrees of blackness possible in the human race. By 1555, in books like Richard Eden's *Decades*, which included accounts of voyages to the dark continent, there were available first-hand descriptions of 'Moors, Moorens, or Negroes' and evidence that some could be of noble and even royal blood. And in 1601 Africans were to be seen in sufficient numbers in London for Queen Elizabeth to be 'discontented at the great numbers of Negars and blackamoors which are crept into the realm'.

As the knowledge of the dark continent became more widespread, under the influence of Hakluyt's *Principal Navigations* (1589), distinctions drawn between various African peoples were possible. For example, George Abbott, in *A Brief Description of the Whole World* (1599), separated 'blackish Moors' from 'exceedingly black Negroes . . . than whom no men are blacker'; and Leo Africanus underlined the difference with his 'white or tawny Moors' from the Mediterranean coast and the southern 'Negroes or black Moors'. That Shakespeare was aware of such distinctions as these is obvious from the stage direction to 2.1 [act 2, scene 1] of *The Merchant of Venice*, which signals the entrance of the Prince of Morocco as 'a tawny Moor all in white'. Also, like his fellow Londoners, he could compare visually the 'Negars and blackamoors', which so troubled the queen, with the sixteen members of the embassy from Barbary who, led by Abd el-Ouahed ben Messaoud, were in the city between August 1600 and February of the following year. During their stay, their dress, customs and behaviour caused a scandal which must have caught the attention of all Londoners; and there is still extant the official portrait of the ambassador himself, showing a bearded, hawk-faced, cunning Arab complete with turban, flowing robes, and elaborately ornamented scimitar. . . .

Evidence of the Kind of Moor Othello Is

The evidence for the kind of Moor Othello is in the play is far more difficult to interpret; and this has led to the widely different costumes and make-up that actors have adopted for the role. At first sight the references to his colour seem straightforward, with the words of many of the characters being very specific for us today. The Duke assures Brabantio that his 'son-in-law is far more fair than black' (1.3.286); Iago toasts the health of the 'black Othello' (2.3.27); Brabantio finds it incredible that his daughter would cleave to a 'sooty bosom' (1.2.70); Emilia, rising to the defence of her mistress, sees the Moor as a 'blacker devil' (5.2.132); and Othello himself laments, 'haply for I am black' (3.3.265) and sees Desdemona's supposedly besmirched honour as being 'begrimed and black' as his own face (3.3.388–9). But we know that Shakespeare did use the word 'black' to mean 'brunette' (as opposed to 'blonde') or merely 'dark-complexioned' (as opposed to 'fair-skinned, not sun-tanned'), usually in an uncomplimentary sense; though it should be noted that, of some fifty-six occasions on which he uses the word, in only about seven does it have this connotation.

All of the other indications of Othello's race amount to an awareness that his features are strikingly at odds with white

Venetian standards of good looks. To the jealous rival, Roderigo, he is a 'thick-lips' (1.1.67); he is a 'devil' to Emilia
(5.2.132); Iago envisions him as 'an old black ram' (1.1.89),
and as someone at whom the typical Venetian gorge heaves
with disrelish (2.1.221-2). Desdemona herself feels obliged to
account for her rejection of the racial norms of appearance in
her choice of a husband by telling the Senate that she 'saw
Othello's visage in his mind' (1.3.248); even as one element in
her father's disbelief is the conviction that her nature could
not err so preposterously as to wed 'what she feared to look
on' (1.3.98). Perhaps most surprisingly of all, Iago, believing
sincerely that Desdemona must grow to see that her husband
is defective in loveliness of favour (2.1.218–20), is actually able
to get Othello to accept without demur that it proves her unnatural that she refused 'many proposèd matches/Of her own
clime, complexion, and degree' (3.3.231–2), in order to wed
someone whose looks made her shake with fear (3.3.209).

Maybe a Negro, Maybe an Arab

For the modern reader all of these indications of colour and
race would almost certainly point to a Negro; but for the
seventeenth-century Londoner they could apply equally well
to an Arab. Iago's derogatory comparison of Othello to a 'Barbary horse' (1.1. 111–12) would not be taken by any member
of the Blackfriars [Theatre] audience to be other than to an
Arabian steed; and his scornful use of the term 'barbarian'
(1.3.343) is exactly that used by Elizabeth's courtiers to refer
to Abd el-Ouahed and his entourage. Even in the lie he tells
Roderigo about Othello's demotion, it is Mauritania (i.e. the
land of the Moors) he selects for the imaginary posting
(4.2.217). More generally, it was the north African races that
were popularly associated with the kinds of reactions that
Othello manifests in the play: as Leo Africanus writes of the
Moors of Barbary,

OTHELLO

T H E

Moor of Venice.

A

T R A G E D Y,

As it hath been divers times acted at the *Globe,*
and at the *Black-Friers*:

And now at the

THEATER ROYAL,

B Y

HIS MAJESTIES SERVANTS.

Written by *William Shakespear.*

L O N D O N,

Printed for *W Weak,* and are to be fold by *Richard Bent-*
ley and *M. Magnes* in *Ruffel Street* near *Covent-*
Garden, 1681.

Title page to the 1681 quarto edition of Shakespeare's Othello, the Moor of Venice. ©
Bettmann/Corbis.

No nation in the world is so subject unto jealousy; for they will rather lose their lives, than put up any disgrace in the behalf of their women.

There is, then, no way of saying with absolute certainty how Shakespeare conceived Othello racially. A black/white opposition is clearly built into the play at every level: factually, physically, visually, poetically, psychologically, symbolically, morally and religiously. This is ultimately the only important theatrical fact. And being so, it is probably true that, regardless of how such an effect could have been created on the Jacobean stage, only a Negroid Othello can produce the desired responses in the theatres of the Western world, at present and in the foreseeable future.

Contradictory and Shifting Notions of Black and White in *Othello*

Doris Adler

Doris Adler was a professor at Howard University, a historically black university, when this article was published. She has written books on the Elizabethan dramatists Thomas Dekker and Phillip Massinger.

In the following excerpt, Adler notes the terms "black" and "fair" have multiple connotations in Othello, *originating with the identification of the color black and the black race with moral blackness and filth. Black denotes the Moor or Negro and a practitioner of the black arts, she says. Fair is identified with virtue and purity. Black is also associated with Africa and fair with Europe, an attitude prevalent in Elizabethan England. Thus, the union of black and white was regarded as unnatural. But in a reversal, Othello's guileless acceptance of Iago's story of Desdemona's adultery causes Othello to see the white Desdemona as morally black. The moral definitions of color are turned upside down as Bianca, whose name means "white" but who sells her body and would ordinarily have a "black" reputation, is described as white and fair. Othello, upon learning of Desdemona's innocence, changes her color from black to white and takes moral blackness upon himself.*

As a white teacher of black students at Howard University in 1969 when the heightened sensitivity to and the justified rebellion against the pejorative values and racial overtones of *black* in our language and literature had reached an

Doris Adler, "The Rhetoric of Black and White in *Othello*," *Shakespeare Quarterly*, vol. 25, Spring 1974, pp. 248–257. Copyright © 1974 by Johns Hopkins University Press. All rights reserved. Reproduced by permission.

explosive pitch, I found the preparation of *Othello* an arduous but illuminating exercise. The repeated use of the terms *black* and *white*, with various but always polarized meanings, and the relationship of those terms to other suggested and dramatized elements of the play required, indeed demanded, a full explication of the terms and of Shakespeare's use of them in *Othello*. Such an explication suggests that the complex and confusing values of *black* and *white* are used to reinforce the theme of man's tragic blindness in *Othello*. . . .

The Multiple Connotations of Blackness

Within *Othello, black* is used with five explicit denotations, and *white* or *fair* is posed in each instance, either explicitly or by suggestion, as the opposite quality. First, *black* is used as a color designation for the darkest hue, "an old black ram" (I.i.88); *white*, as the opposite, designates the lightest hue: "white ewe" (I.i.89). Second, *black* is used to designate a Moor, a Negro, one of African origin: "the black Othello" (II.ii.29); *white* is suggested for European counterparts, as in Othello's reference to Desdemona, "that whiter skin of hers than snow" (V.ii.4). Third, *black* is used to describe a brunette, "black and witty" (II.i.131), and both *white* and *fair* are used to describe a blond, "fair and wise" (II.i.129), "a white that shall her blackness fit" (II.i.133). Fourth, *black* is used to denote the soil of filth or grime, "Her name . . . is now begrimed and black" (III.iii.386–87), and by suggestion, *white* is clean or unsoiled. Fifth, and finally, *black* is used for the morally foul: "blackest sins" (II.iii.334), "black vengeance" (III.iii.447); and *fair* is used as an aspect of virtue: "If virtue no delighted beauty lack,/Your son-in-law is far more fair than black" (I.iii.289–90).

While only two of the meanings of black—literally soiled or morally foul—evoke a specifically negative response, the other meanings had accumulated negative connotations that Shakespeare could draw on. The proverbial black sheep, the black and burning pit of hell, and the black devil of legend, illustration, and dramatic representation served as elements to combine the meanings of *black* as a simple color designation and *black* both as grime or filth and as morally foul. Shakespeare draws on these associative values when he has Emilia say to Othello, "And you the blacker devil!" (V.ii.130). He further stresses and reinforces the evil values of the color *black* by using "the black sheep" in the grossly sexual image, "Even now, now, very now, an old black ram/Is tupping your white ewe" (I.i.88–89), and by using the ominous black bird of evil omen: "As doth the raven o'er the infected house/Boding to all!" (IV.i.21–22).

"Black" a Negative Term in Elizabethan England

Black as a racial designation, like *black* the color, was a negatively charged word. Even without Eldred D. Jones' excellent account of the Elizabethan view of Africans, many of the ingredients of the pejorative stereotype of the African are discernible in *Othello*. The African is considered ugly,

such a thing as thou, to fear, not to delight

(I.ii.71)

For nature so preposterously to err

Being not deficient, blind, or lame of sense,

(I.iii.62–63)

lascivious,

To the gross clasps of a lascivious Moor,

(I.i.127)

an unnatural mate for a European,

Not to affect many propos'd matches

Of her own clime, complexion, and degree,

Whereto we see in all things nature tends—

(III.iii.229–31)

a practitioner of forbidden arts,

Thou hast enchanted her,

(I.ii.63)

of a volatile, even savage nature,

Dangerous conceits are in their natures poisons;

Which at the first are scarce found to distaste,

But with a little act upon the blood

Burn like the mines of sulphur,

(III.iii.326–29)

and clearly not as polished or as cultivated as Europeans of a similar class,

Haply, for I am black

And have not those soft parts of conversation

That chamberers have.

(III.iii.263–64)

Black Is Confounded and Intensified Whenever Used

Obviously these are not the attributes of Othello, who is attractive enough to win Desdemona, of such a continent nature that he considers "the young affects/In me defunct"

(I.iii.263–64), of such a "constant, loving, noble nature" that even Iago thinks "he'll prove to Desdemona/A most dear husband" (II.i.283–85), practitioner only of the magic art of winning words, at which he has clearly surpassed his Venetian rivals, and no more subject to lethal passion than Cassio or Roderigo, both of whom are incited to violence by Iago. . . .

The third designated meaning, *black* as a dark-haired person, like the first two, also connotes qualities or values which are the result of taste or preference rather than the inherent qualities of the class designated. The *black*, or brunette, was considered less attractive, less fortunate, than the *fair*, or blond. According to Iago, "If she be black, and thereto have a wit/She'll find a white that shall her blackness fit" (II.i.132–33). Unlike the fair, she will have to use wit to find a suitable mate. In addition, the *black* in this passage is made to share connotations of *black* as literally and morally unclean by means of a rhetorical exchange of terms. In the interchange between Desdemona and Iago, Iago is charged to praise first the "fair and witty," then the "black and witty," then the "fair and foolish," and, lastly, not the expected "black and foolish," but, instead, the "foul and foolish" (II.i.129–35). *Foul* as a synonym for *black* as either literally or morally unclean is substituted for *black* as a brunette with the effect of making the earlier uses of *black* equivocal. The substitution of one meaning of *black* for another, the equivocal use of synonymous terms, and the yoking of attributes of one meaning of *black* with those of a different meaning of *black* are used throughout the play with the effect of confounding and intensifying the value of *black* whenever it is used in any sense.

Blackness as Filth and Mixed Marriage as Unnatural

When the audience meets the noble Moor, his blackness has been verbally linked with ugliness, the strange and unnatural, gross animal sensuality, and the evil of the devil himself.

Brabantio reinforces the negative associations when he confronts Othello by applying a synonym for *black* as dirty to the racially *black* Othello, "O thou foul thief" (I.ii.62); by assuming that black Othello like the black devil is damned, "Damned as thou art" (I.ii.63); by assuming that Othello, in compliance with the stereotype, has used forbidden arts, "thou hast enchanted her" (I.ii.63); and by stressing his own support of the general belief in the unnaturalness of the union of black and white,

> For I'll refer me to all things of sense. . . .
>
> Whether a maid so tender, fair, and happy. . . .
>
> Would ever have, t'incur a general mock. . . .
>
> (I.ii.64,66,69)

Fair, in this passage, is ambiguous; is Desdemona white, blond, beautiful, virtuous, or all of these? Brabantio adds the quality of soiled or dirty to the already overloaded significance of Othello's blackness in the passage, "Run from her guardage to the sooty bosom" (I.ii.70), further stresses the association of Othello and the devil by apprehending Othello in terms more applicable to the devil, "For an abuser of the world, a practicer/Of arts inhibited and out of warrant" (I.ii.78–79), and combines the associations of ugliness, unnaturalness, and the diabolical.

Othello Calls Desdemona Black

With the negative values of *black* and the positive values of *white* fully established, Iago gives warning that foul will seem fair, and fair will seem foul; black will seem white, and white will seem black.

Until this point in the play, only those with self-serving reasons have viewed Othello as metaphorically black: Roderigo, Iago, and Brabantio. From this point in the play, when

Iago begins to exploit Othello's tragic blindness, Othello begins to describe himself in terms of the racial stereotype, and to describe Desdemona as metaphorically black. After describing Desdemona in terms that suggest the whiteness of skin, beauty, and virtue, "To say my wife is fair, feeds well, loves company . . . /Where virtue is, these are more virtuous" (III.iii.183,185), Othello, himself, suggests their union was unnatural: "And yet, how nature erring from itself" (III.iii.227). Iago, catching the edge of Othello's self-doubt, and blackening Desdemona's virtuous appetite, sets forth the full ugly image which Othello is ready to accept as reality. . . .

After a moment of doubt that anyone so literally fair could be metaphorically black, "If she be false, O, then heaven mocks itself" (III.iii.278), Othello draws on the blackness of filth to describe Desdemona's name and his own face:

Her name, that was as fresh

As Dian's visage, is now begrimed and black

As mine own face.

(III.iii.286–89)

Othello calls for, "black vengeance, from the hollow hell" (III.iii.447), swears "by yond marble heaven" (III.iii.460), evoking the image of both whiteness and hardness, and like the black and evil devil asks for means to kill the white-skinned black devil:

Damn her, lewd minx! O, damn her! damn her!

Come, go with me apart. I will withdraw

To furnish me with some swift means of death

For the fair devil.

(III.iii.476–79)

Othello, so often called devil himself throughout the early part of the play, now uses "devil" repeatedly in reference to Desdemona. On taking her hand, he comments, "For here's a young and sweating devil here/That commonly rebels" (III.iv.42–43). He cries, "O devil" (IV.i.43), as he falls into a trance after reiterating the ingredients of his poisoned vision of her. He calls her "Devil" as he strikes her before Lodovico (IV.i.233), and repeats, "O devil, devil!" (IV.i.237), as he sends her from them. When he finally comes to confront Desdemona with his irrational accusations, he does so in terms of damnation and devils. . . .

The battery of negative connotations of black used in contrast to the beauty of whiteness against Othello in Act I is now used by him in his tirade against Desdemona. . . .

Contrary Uses of Black and White

Othello, the black-skinned, is called "fair" by the Duke; Desdemona, the fair-skinned, is called "black" by Othello; Bianca, who is described as, "A huswife that by selling her desires/Buys herself bread and clothes" (IV.i.94–95), bears a name that means "white," and is called the "most fair Bianca" (III.iv.171) by Cassio. Bianca has the blackened reputation Iago would give to Desdemona, yet she is called "white" and "fair." A fair whore, named Bianca, is a further complication in the dramatic rhetoric of *black* and *white*.

Desdemona's whiteness—literal, beautiful, and metaphorical—is nowhere more powerfully evoked than in Othello's lines before he kills her:

Yet I'll not shed her blood

Nor scar that whiter skin of hers than snow,

And smooth as monumental alabaster.

(V.ii.3–5)

British actor Sir Johnston Forbes-Robertson performs the role of Othello in blackface, circa 1895. © Hulton-Deutsch Collection/Corbis.

Only with the full realization of Desdemona's innocence and his own guilt does Othello see Desdemona's whiteness as heavenly, and he then commends himself to the blackness of hell and devils. The whiteness of her face and dress, the coldness that suggests the whiter snow, the unblemished chastity, the fairness of the heavenly sight, are contrasted with the blackness of fiends, devils, and hell itself. . . .

Othello's blackness is now neither African nor devil, but that of the victim, damned to hell. . . .

Much that man has been taught to believe, such as being able to identify the devil by his cloven hoofs, is fable: black is not always evil, but black can be evil; all called white are not fair, but some are lovely fair. . . .

Black and white are used with the confused values of fable and reality: it is a fable that the devil is black, yet black Othello is damned by killing his wife; it is a fable that white is the color of virtue, the fair Bianca is a whore, and yet the virtuous Desdemona is lovely fair. *Black* and *white*, used with the confused values of fable and reality, reinforce, rhetorically, the tragic theme of *Othello*.

Sexuality and Racial Difference

Ania Loomba

Ania Loomba, an English professor at the University of Pennsylvania, is the author of books on colonialism and postcolonialism, including Shakespeare, Race, and Colonialism.

In the following essay, excerpted from the original, Looma wants to get across the fact that she is writing from the perspective of an Indian woman of color. Historically, she writes, skin colors had moral implications, black meaning satanic, as opposed to fair meaning morally good. This view, supported by scripture, was prevalent in William Shakespeare's England. Added to this racism was the economic threat that black people posed to white workers, part of Queen Elizabeth's argument to the Privy Council, seeking deportation of blacks. In this atmosphere, Shakespeare makes a black man the tragic hero of his play, startling his English audiences. In the beginning of Othello's career in Venice, he is an accepted member of the white patriarchy, but racism rears its head with his romantic connection to a white woman. He is then regarded as having demonic magical powers over her. Iago, in his rivalry and jealousy of Othello, stereotypes Othello as repulsive and Desdemona as degenerate.

[C]ardiff University professor, philosopher, and critic] Christopher Norris has pointed out that, despite variations, *Othello* criticism from [Samuel] Johnson to [F.R.] Leavis can be seen as part of 'a certain dominant cultural formation in the history of Shakespeare studies. It is an effort of ideological containment, an attempt to harness the unruly energies of the text to a stable order of significance' (p. 66). I suggest

Ania Loomba, *Gender, Race, Renaissance Drama*. Manchester, UK: Manchester University Press, 1989, 38–64. Copyright © 1989 by Ania Loomba. All rights reserved. Reproduced by permission of the author.

that this stable order, could only be invoked by the simultaneous exclusion of both gender and race; therefore, firstly, as a recent feminist essay points out, both 'Othello critics' (who sentimentalise Othello) and 'Iago critics' (who emphasise Iago's realism and 'honesty') 'badly misunderstand and misrepresent the women in the play' (Neely, p. 212), and secondly, as Ruth Cowhig indicates, the question of race is 'largely ignored by critical commentaries' (p. 8).[2] In 1693, Thomas Rymer interpreted the play as 'a caution to all Maidens of Quality, how, without their parents' consent they run away with Blackamoors . . .' (p. 89). This combined a patriarchal view of female waywardness and the necessity of obedience, a racist warning against the rampant sexuality of black men, and a class consciousness which prioritises the submission of women 'of Quality'. Nearly 300 years later, Leslie Fiedler, among the first in recent times to acknowledge the connections between racial and sexual themes, argues that Othello moves from being a stranger whose colour establishes his difference ('cultural' rather than ethnic) to becoming, towards the end of the play, 'colourless: a provincial gentleman-warrior, a downright English soldier fallen among foreigners; which means that he no longer functions archetypally even as a stranger, mush less a black' (p. 160). For this downfall of the inwardly white Othello, Desdemona the 'white witch' and Iago the true black are jointly held responsible. Emelia is 'first and last an untamed shrew' and generally, the women 'by their lives and functions . . . seem rather to sustain Iago's view of women' (p. 141).

It is a measure of the problem I want to highlight that although Carole Neely criticises Fiedler's misogyny, she both ignores his racism (which is less crude than Rymer's or Ridley's but there nevertheless) and makes no attempt to analyse the impact of Othello's blackness on the sexual relations in the play.[3] To address sexual difference at the expense of the racial is to produce what Newton and Rosenfelt have called 'a feminist version of "the" human condition' (p. xvii) which is especially invalid for women in the 'third world', who are at the juncture of both sorts of oppression. Although the question of race has been admirably discussed recently (see Cowhig and Orkin's essays), it is often ignored or underplayed even by those concerned with alternative and political criticism, and has not been fully inserted into discussions of gender difference.[4]

In a brief article, Ben Okri points out that 'to reduce the colour is to diminish the force of the sex. Working together they can be quite unbearable' (p. 563). Even though no simple mapping of racial difference on to the sexual is possible precisely because Othello's colour and gender make him occupy contradictory positions in relation to power, I shall suggest that firstly, Othello's blackness is central to any understanding of male or female sexuality or power structures in the play; secondly, the filtering of sexuality and race through each other's prism profoundly affects each of them, thus indicating more clearly what Lentricchia has called the 'multiplicity of histories' of both authority and resistance; and thirdly, such interweaving does not *dissolve* the tensions between different forms of oppression but acknowledges and addresses them, as well as placing the schisms and discontinuities of identity (which recent criticism has seen foregrounded in Renaissance drama; see Dollimore, *Radical Tragedy*, and Belsey, *The Subject of Tragedy*) within the neglected context of racial difference.

Historicising Racism

It had been a major problem for critics of the play to reconcile Othello's blackness with his central position in the play. Therefore either his colour was ignored, or much critical effort was expended in trying to prove that Shakespeare did not intend him to be black at all (see Cowhig, p. 16). Both views are premised upon racist notions of black inferiority. The notion that 'all men are the same' includes the apparently conflicting one that 'blacks are inferior, and hardly men at all'. [M.R.] Ridley's efforts to prove Othello's non-negroid racial origins are notoriously and crudely racist: 'There are more colours than one in Africa, and that a man is black in colour is no reason why he should, even to European eyes, look subhuman' (p. li). Then we also hear that 'for Shakespeare, "black" does not describe an ethnic distinction . . . "fair" has a primarily moral significance'; that there was no racism in Elizabethan England, that the kind of horror that contemporary audiences might feel at a black/white mating is therefore no part of the play; that since 'miscegenation had not yet been invented' we are to read the blackness of Othello as 'primarily symbolic' and finally, 'it is no real surprise, therefore, to discover that Othello was not ethnically "black at all" in the sources from which Cinthio drew his story' (Fiedler, pp. 143–5). It is no surprise either to discover that Fiedler's moral categories quickly slide back to ethnic ones. How colours come to be invested with moral connotations is precisely the history of racism.

Evidence of such a history during Elizabethan times has been accumulating, and here I will only amplify aspects that crucially link it with the question of gender. [Critic] G.K. Hunter identifies a 'powerful and ancient tradition associating black-faced men with wickedness . . . (which) came right up to Shakespeare's own day' (p. 35). Part of this tradition derived from a Bible-centred conception of the world in which humanity was graded according to its geographical distance from the Holy Land—hence black people were devilish because they existed outside both the physical and the conceptual realm of Christianity. Blacks became identified with the descendants of [Noah's son] Ham, and their colour a direct consequence of sexual excess. The devil and his associates, even in Reginald Scott's fairly rationalist *The Discovery of Witchcraft*, were inextricably linked with blackness: 'a damned soul may and doth take the shape of a blackamoore' (Hunter, p. 34).

Hunter also includes a general cultural hostility to strangers as a factor influencing racial prejudice, but erroneously locates this to 'a response to the basic antinomy of day and night' which to him explains the presence of racism 'all over the world (even in darkest Africa) from the earliest to the latest times'. This dangerously universalises and naturalises white racism, whose various histories indicate interlinking situations of oppression rather than a trans-historical colour consciousness. Eldred Jones's pioneering study *Othello's Countrymen* established that Shakespeare did not depend on literary sources for his portraits of black people and that there was a growing black presence in England with evidence of its widening contact with white inhabitants. Hakluyt's *Principal Navigations* bears witness to the beginnings of slave trade: between 1562 and 1568, Hawkins brought 'blackamoors to England' and sold hundreds of black slaves to Spain, so there were 'several hundreds of black people living in households of the aristocracy and the landed gentry' (Cowhig, p. 5).

Thus, Hunter's arguments that Elizabethans had 'no continuous contact' with black people and 'no sense of economic threat from them' (p. 32) are historically disproved. But the crucial point is that the black presence was both perceived and constructed as a threat by the state. Royal proclamations and state papers nervously point to the 'great numbers of negroes and blackamoors in the country, of which kind of people there are already too manye'. Queen Elizabeth's correspondence with the Privy Council, seeking to deport eighty-nine black people, is significant. A warrant issued on 18 July 1596 contrasts black or 'those kinde of people' with her white subjects or 'Christian people' in a passage startlingly illustrative of the Orientalist split between a superior European culture, constituting 'us', and the inferior non-European peoples and cultures, constituting 'them'. This split, as Said has argued, is a crucial component in establishing the hegemony of the former (*Orientalism*, p. 7). But Elizabeth's communiqué also crucially puts forward the argument that blacks will create unemployment, 'want of service', for her white people. Here again she evokes the myth of a rampant black sexuality and their 'populous' numbers, seeking to limit and control black presence in the imperial country (quoted Cowhig, p. 6).[5]. . .

'Ravenous Tigers' and 'Inhuman Dogs'

Cowhig points out that 'only as we recognise the familiarity of the figure of the black man as villain in Elizabethan drama can we appreciate what must have been the startling impact on Shakespeare's audience of a black hero' (pp. 4–5). Shakespeare made significant departures from his source material, from other representations of blacks on the Renaissance stage, and from his own earlier portraits of Moors (as both Hunter and cowhig have shown). The tradition of the black villain-hero in Elizabethan drama resulted in a series of negative portrayals of black men, such as Muly Mahomet in Thomas Peele's *The Battle of Alcazar* or Eleazor in *Lust's Dominion*, written by [Thomas] Dekker and others. In Shakespeare's *Love's Labour Lost*, 'Black is the badge of hell/The hue of dungeons and the school of night' (IV.iii.250–1). In Cinthio's version of the Othello story, his 'blackness already displeases' Desdemona, and Othello carefully plots how to murder her without being caught. Hunter points out that Shakespeare changes many features of Cinthio's tale, but not the colour of the hero. A brief look at Shakespeare's earlier fullest treatment of race in *Titus Andronicus* reveals the extent to which *Othello* departs from the usual linkage of black men with deviant white women. . . .

In *Othello*, I shall suggest, commonsense ideas about blacks are evoked but more clearly questioned, disclosed as misrepresentation. And, crucially, this disclosure is closely interwoven with the disturbance to patriarchal authority. . . .

Racism / Patriarchalism

I will locate a movement which is precisely the opposite of the one seen by Fiedler and will trace Othello's passage from an honorary white to a total outsider, a movement that depends on the impact of both racial and sexual difference.[6] In other words, Othello moves from being a colonised subject existing on the terms of white Venetian society and trying to internalise its ideology, towards being marginalised, outcast and alienated from it in every way until he occupies his 'true' position as its other. His precarious entry into the white world is ruptured by his relation with Desdemona, which was intended to secure it in the first place, and which only catalyses the contradictions in Othello's self-conception. So instead of the unified subject of humanist thought, we have a near schizophrenic hero whose last speech graphically portrays the split—he becomes simultaneously the Christian and the Infidel, the Venetian and the Turk, the keeper of the State and its opponent. At the same time, Desdemona passes from being his ally who would guarantee his white status to becoming his sexual and racial 'other'. As will be dicsussed later, she too is a split, inconsistent subject and occupies not one but various positions in the play, not only as Othello's 'other' but also that of the Venetian patriarchy.

The 'central conflict' of the play then, if we must locate one, is neither between white and black alone, nor merely between men and women—it is rather between the racism of a white patriarchy and the threat posed to it by both a black man and a white woman. But these two are not simply aligned against white patriarchy, since their own relation cannot be abstracted from sexual or racial tension. Othello is not merely a black man who is jealous, but a man whose jealousy and blackness are inseparable. Similarly, Desdemona's initial boldness and later submission are not discordant in the context of her positions as a *white* woman and a white *woman*. There is thus a tripartite and extremely complex relationship between black man, white woman, and the state.

In the first 125 lines of the play, racist images of Othello's blackness abound—he is 'thick lips', 'old black ram', 'a Barbary

horse', 'devil' and 'a lascivious Moor'. It is significant that, unlike Aaron's case, these images are evoked almost exclusively in
the context of his contact with a white woman, which transforms the latent racism of Venetian society into Brabantio's
virulent anger and Iago's digust. From honoured guest to that
of an inhuman Othello becomes 'such a thing as thou' (I.ii.71)
whose liaison is 'against all rules of nature' (I.iii.101) (see
Cowhig, p. 8). Brabantio's conviction that Othello has used
magic to win her at once dislodges Othello to the status of a
barbaric outsider, an animal whom he claims his daughter was
afraid to look upon. Here Othello is associated with an activity with overwhelmingly female connotations, i.e. witchcraft.
Cleopatra too, it may be recalled, is accused of magically en-
chanting Antony. But Cleopatra's feminine wiles are specifically linked to her being an Egyptian and we are reminded
that sorcery is repeatedly constructed as being an uncivilised
and un-Christian activity as well, in themselves Othello and
Cleopatra cannot be sexually attractive.

Constructing the Other

Othello is a Moor, but there is no real clarity as to his precise
origins despite references to his being sold in slavery and to
his un-Christian past. Debates over whether Othello was black,
brown or mulatto anxiously tried to recover the possibility of
his whiteness from this ambiguity, which, on the contrary,
alerts us to the very construction of the 'other' in Orientalist
and colonial discourses.While we must recognise that each
non-white race or group has an individual identity, a unifor-
mity is conferred upon them by there common differentiation
from white civilisation. Robinson notes that 'prior to the elev-
enth or twelfth centuries the use of the collective sense of the
term barbarian was primarily a function of exclusion rather
than a reflection of any significant consolidation among these
peoples' (p. 10). Thus to consider Othello as a black man is
not to gloss over the textual confusion but to concur with

Fanon that colonial discourse itself erases differentiation between various subjects and treats all outsiders as black; while locating its racism therefore, we need to stress the common exclusion of its 'others', whose political colour rather than precise shade of non-whiteness is what matters.

The conversion of the outsider to the service of dominant culture is a crucial feature of the European encounter with other peoples. Hence the alien must also be incorporated (Said, *Orientalism*, p. 71). Othello is valuable as a Christian warrior, or the exotic colonial subject in the service of the state. In the Senate scene, the Venetian patriarchy displays an amazing capacity to variously construct, co-opt and exclude its 'others'. Brabantio is certain that the Senate will back his opposition to Othello's marriage, and if it appears strange (or remarkably liberal) that they don't, we need only to recall their concern with the Turkish threat. Othello the warrior is strategically included as one of 'us' as opposed to the Turkish 'they': 'You must therefore be content to slubber the gloss of your new fortunes with this more stubborn and boisterous expedition' (I.iii.227–8).

Iago's famous 'motiveless malignity' (as Coleridge called it) according to Greenblatt still 'remains opaque' (*Renaissance Self-Fashioning*, p. 236). This is partly because many of Iago's statements are often regarded as irrational, and as evidence of his almost mythic, hardly human wickedness. The following passage is often cited as an example of such illogical behaviour:

. . . Now I do love her too;

Not out of absolute lust, though peradventure

I stand accountant for as great a sin

But partly led to diet my revenge,

For that I do suspect the lustful Moor

Hath leap'd into my seat, the thought whereof

Doth like a poisonous mineral gnaw my inwards;

And nothing can, nor shall content my soul

Till I am even'd with him, wife for wife . . .
(II.i.285–93)

In what sense does Iago love Desdemona? Does he really suspect Emilia with Othello? Rather than confusion of motive, the passage illustrates the way in which sexual desire is expressive of a power struggle here in a specifically racist context. Iago 'loves' Desdemona in the same as Ferdinand loves his sister, the Duchess of Malfi. In the latter case, erotic desire, brotherly possessiveness and male authoritarianism blend as expressions of aristocratic bonding, and of protection of state and family power. Similarly Iago's 'love' speaks of a racial and patriarchal bonding whereby he becomes the 'protector' of all white women from black men. More specifically, as a white woman, Desdemona belongs to him rather than to Othello. Such possessiveness over all white women is also reflected in the fear (rationalised as 'suspicion') of losing his wife to Othello.

As Cowhig indicates, Iago's disgust at Desdemona's choice reveals an almost phobic racist horror:

Not to affect many proposed matches,

Of her own clime, complexion and degree,

Whereto we see in all things nature tends—

Foh! one may smell in such a will most rank,

Foul disproportion, *thoughts unnatural.*
(III.iii.233–7; emphasis added) . . .

Iago, played by Kenneth Branagh, speaks to Othello, played by Laurence Fishburne, in a 1995 film adaptation of Othello *directed by Oliver Parker.* © Castle Rock/Dakota Films/ The Kobal Collection/Rolf Konow.

This interchange between Iago and Othello allows us to see that the 'naturalness' which dominant ideologies invoke to legitimise themselves and which is central to common-sense thinking generally, is a flexible category. For Othello, seeking to efface his own blackness through Desdemona's love, a patriarchal view of female constancy as 'natural' is necessary. Therefore for him Desdemona's supposed dishonesty becomes 'nature erring from itself (III.iii.231). But Iago reinterprets erring nature to define Desdemona as a white woman, whose love for and constancy to Othello is 'unnatural'. So he yokes together stereotypical notions of both 'black' as repulsive and 'female' as ever-capable of unnatural transgressions.

As Lawrence correctly points out, whereas the rapes of black women by white men were seen as a sort of favour to the black race, the mating of white women with black men was regarded as fatal. Whereas the first extended the power of the white man over all women, the latter eroded his own territory, and allowed for the possibility of its 'invasion'. In the

Indian context, British (and other colonial) men indulged in widespread sexual liaisons with (including rapes of) Indian women as a matter of course. But the horrors of British women taking on Indian lovers are obsessively foregrounded in literature as diverse as Forster's *A Passage to India*, Paul Scott's *The Raj Quarter* and Jhabvala's *Heat and Dust*; they persist as a feature of contemporary racism: 'in Britain today, the question is never: would you allow your son to marry a black girl? It is always: would you allow your daughter to marry a black man?' (Lawrence, 'Just plain common-sense', p. 72). Such a nexus of the fears evoked by black and active female sexuality is responsible for engendering the extreme horrors of *Titus Andronicus*, where it results in racial pollution. From Elizabeth I's communique deporting blacks, referred to earlier, to today's British immigration laws. The 'preservation' of the white race is seen to be at stake. Fanon offered a psychoanalytical explanation for this fear, pointing out that racist phobia always reduces the black man to his sexual potential: the father revolts because in his opinion the Negro will introduce his daughter into a sexua universe for which the father does not have the key, the weapons, or the attributes' (p. 165).

So what is especially threatening for white patriarchy is the possibility of the *complicity* of white women; their desire for black lovers is feared, forbidden, but always imminent. The spectre of a combined black and female insubordination 'threatens to undermine white manhood and the Empire at a stroke' (Lawrence, p. 64). The effort then becomes to project the white woman's desire as provoked by the animalistic lust of the black man, a notion which is traceable as far back as the fifteenth century in Europe and much earlier in India. The myth of the black rapist is even more useful for it perpetuates black animalism while obliterating female agency, and thus simultaneously 'erases' the two most problematic areas for patriarchal racism—the humanity of the alien race and the active sexuality of women.

Even if she is passive, however, the white woman's contact with the alien male pollutes her. In chapter 6, the black man's supposed rapacity will be further discussed in the context of *The Tempest*. But in *Othello* the problem arises precisely because Othello is not a rapist and Desdemona is not an unwilling victim of his sexual assault. Their desire cannot be contained within the myth of the black rapist. In spite of this, Iago's racism and his misogyny together make him confident that the 'relation between an erring barbarian and a supersubtle Venetian' can be easily disrupted (I.iii.356).

'Haply for I Am Black'

Othello is described in terms of the characteristics popularly attributed to blacks during the sixteenth century: sexual potency, courage, pride, guilelessness, credulity, easily aroused passions; these become central and persistent features of later colonial stereotyping as well, as I remarked in the first chapter. At the beginning of the play he is seemingly well entrenched in and accepted by Venetian society—an honorary white, whose hyperbolic speech is an attempt to speak better than any the language of his adoptive civilisation (see Serpieri, p. 142). The vulnerability of his entry prompts him to reiterate his intrinsic merits, his lineage and his achievements; he appears confident that these will match Brabantio's racism:

> My services which I have done the signiory
>
> Shall out-tongue his complaints . . . (I.ii.18–
> 19)

Othello needs to believe that 'my parts, my tide and my perfect soul/Shall manifest me rightly' (I.ii.31–2). He is to discover that the dominant ideology encouraged by his adoptive society, especially the notion of the power and indestructible essence of the individual, is doubly illusory when your skin is black.

But if Othello is not archetypal man, neither is he simply *any* black man. The drama of racial difference is played out on spaces already occupied by divisions of class. He is involved in the process of social mobility and self-fashioning as are others around him, but on somewhat different terms. Brecht rightly pointed out that

> he doesn't only possess Desdemona, he also possesses a post as general, which he has not inherited as a feudal general would, but won by outstanding achievements, and presumably snatched from someone else; he must defend it or it will be snatched from him. He lives in a world of fighting for property and position, and his relationship with the woman he loves develops as a property relationship. (quoted Heinemann, p. 217)

Iago is jealous of Cassio's preferment and also of Othello, who is more successful in their common pursuit of status. Iago gains considerable wealth from duping Roderigo: 'I have wasted myself out of my means. The jewels you have had from me to deliver to Desdemona would half have corrupted a votarist' (IV.ii.186–88).

However, class differences cannot he sealed off from others, as Stuart Hall has pointed out in the context of contemporary Britain: 'Race', he says, 'is the modality in which class relations are experienced' (quoted Gilroy, p. 276). Applied to *Othello*, this illuminates the profound invasion, intensification and alteration of class or gender relations by race. Iago's jealousy of Cassio's advancement does not become deflected into hatred for Othello, as is sometimes supposed. Rather, each breeds the other, for Othello is the racial inferior who is socially superior, the outsider who has become the means of Iago's own preferment. Greenblatt has persuasively and correctly argued that Iago's ability to improvise and control events and the lives of others should be located as an effect of colonial ideology which seeks to 'sustain indefinitely indirect enslavement' by moulding the psyche of the oppressed (Greenblatt, *Renaissance Self-Fashioning*, p. 229). But we need to add that such an ideology is not just generally imbibed but shaped and spurred by Iago's specific experience of racial hatred.

Desdemona is both her father's 'jewel' (I.iii.195) and her husband's 'purchase' (II.iii.9). As the guarantee of her husband's upward mobility, she is similar to Bianca (*Women Beware Women*). But unlike the latter, Desdemona is also the gate to white humanity. Slowly his conception of his own worth comes to centre in the fact that she chose him over all the 'curl'd darlings' of Venice. Her desire for him—'for she had eyes, and chose me' (III.iii.193)—replaces his heritage or exploits as proof and measure of his worth. It thus becomes the primary signifier of his identity; that is why 'my life upon her faith' (I.iii.294) and 'when I love thee not, / Chaos is come again' (III.iii.92–3). That is why if she loves him not, 'Farewell! Othello's occupation's gone' (III.iii.361). . . .

Desdemona's Obedience

Othello needs to encourage Desdemona's sexual freedom up to the point that it ensures his own mobility but also subsequently to curb it. He is proud of her speech in the beginning of the play, for it confers a power and a legitimacy on him. Later he smothers her voice for she must speak and move on his behalf only and not when it is suspected that he is not the object of her passion—'O curse of marriage, / That we can call these delicate creatures ours, / And not their appetites' (III.iii.272–4). This is not a general male dilemma however: if we take into account the importance of Desdemona for Othello's entire existence in white society, then the power of the misogynist idea of the changeability, duplicity and frailty of women to rouse and disturb Othello and his vulnerability to Iago's tales of female inconstancy become clearer. He has begun to feel the limits of self-fashioning for a black man in a white world.

At each point that women's frailty is impressed upon Othello, it is in conjunction with his own blackness. Brabantio is the first to plant the possibility of Desdemona's duplicity in Othello's mind ('She has deceiv'd her father and may thee', I.iii.293) which is picked up by Iago later;

She did deceive her father, marrying you;

And when she seem'd to shake and fear your
looks,

She lov'd them most. (III.iii.210–12)

The interweaving of misogyny and racism in Iago's later speeches cannot be missed. Women, in his opinion, are capable of the most unnatural acts, such as loving black men, and the greatest fickleness, such as ceasing to love them. By asking Othello to acknowledge this he both questions Othello's humanity and appeals to his manhood: 'Are you a man? Have you a soul or sense?' (III.iii.378); 'Would you would bear your fortune like a man'; 'Good sir, be a man'; 'Marry, patience; / Or I shall say you are all in all in spleen / And nothing of a man' (IV.i.61, 65, 87–9). The more he questions Othello's humanity, the more he appeals to his masculine power over women. Promising to kill Cassio, he begs Othello to 'let her live', although Othello has up to that time never hinted at killing Desdemona. Just as Othello's white identity was dependent upon Desdemona's love, his destruction of her involves a belief in women's frailty which helps him 'rationalise' her supposed infidelity. Desdemona begins to embody the common patriarchal dichotomy of the white devil. For Othello, this is the only way to yoke together the otherwise contradictory experiences of being black and a man. . . .

Notes

2 I am indebted to Cowhig's essay; despite the fact than she concentrates on the neglect of race in *Othello* criticism, whenever she does mention gender relations she relates

them to racial politics. I am also indebted to Errol
Lawrence's analysis of common sense racist assumptions,
which, along with Fanon, illuminates several aspects of the
play.

3 Both views, then—of Othello as an archetypal man and
as a black man—are premised upon racist notions of black
inferiority. We might assume that crudity such as Ridley's
is somewhat passé, but its assumptions are traceable in
more sophisticated accounts. Fiedler, for example, ends up
asserting Othello's essential, moral whiteness and Iago's
status as the true black. Ridley's arguments, although in
other respects very different, similarly oscillate between
rescuing Othello from the status of a black (he may be
African but is he altogether negroid?), arguing for his inherent inferiority (he is somewhat deficient in reason and
intellect though a warm, loving, instinctual creature), and
thoroughly ignoring Desdemona (he evaluates her worth
by the dignity with which she faces men who have seen
her publicly struck).

4 Karen Newman's article, "'And wash the Ethiop white'"
and Martin Orkin's book, *Shakespeare Against Apartheid*
both make significant departures (in different directions)
from previous criticism of the play. I saw them at a very
late stage in the production of this project, so I am unable
to comment on them fully. Newman's article is unique in
beginning to interrelate racial and sexual difference, and
Orkin brings together the contexts of production and reception—so both together discuss many of my own concerns here. I differ from Orkin's assessment of the Venetian
Senate: 'no evidence emerges in the detail of the language
to suggest that they share a hidden racist disapprobation of
Othello (p. 65). I also think that to say that 'Othello, Desdemona and Cassio seek only love and honor in the play'
(p. 88) is to gloss over the ways in which they are them-

selves 'flawed' by the racial structures; we need to guard against viewing any of them as simple opposition to a racist Iago.

Even otherwise radical critics have not purged their language of the racist moral connotations commonly attached to colour: Greenblatt, for example, speaks of the 'dark essence of Iago's whole enterprise' or the 'unfathomable darkness of human motives' (*Renaissance Self-Fashioning*, pp. 233, 251). It should be noted that such 'slips' coexist with an explicit devaluation of race as a theoretical parameter, which I will discuss shortly. Eagleton's discussion of the play (*William Shakespeare*) takes almost no account of Othello's colour.

5 Elizabeth's communique (quoted by Cowhig, p. 6) reads:

An open warrant to the Lord maiour of London and to all Vice-Admyralls, Maiours and other publicke officers whatsoever to whom yt may appertaine. Whereas Casper van Senden, a merchant of Lubeck, did by his labor and travell procure 89 of her Majesty's subjects that were detayned prisoners in Spaine and Portugall to be released, and brought them hither into the realme at his owne cost and charges, for the which his expenses and declaration of his honest minde towards those prisoners he only desireth to have lycense to take up so much blackamoores here in this realme and to transport them into Spaine and Portugall. Her Majesty in regard to the charitable affection the suppliant hath showed being a stranger, to worke the delivery of our countrymen that were there in great great misery and thraldom and to bring them home to their native country, and that the same could not be done without great expense, and also considering the reasonableness of his requestes to transport so many blackamoores from hence, doth thincke yt a very good exchange and that those kinde of people may well be spared in this realme, being so populous and numbers of hable persons the subjects of the land and Christian people that perishe for want of service, whereby through their labor they might be mayntained. They are therefore in their Lordship's name required to aide and assist him to take up suche blackamoores as he shall finde within this realme with the consent of their masters, who we doubt not, considering her Majesty's good pleasure to have those kinde of people sent out of her lande and the good deserving of the stranger towardes her Majesty's subjectes, and that they shall doe charitably and like Christians rather to be served by their owne countrymen then with those kinde of people, will yielde those in their possession to him.

6 I use the term 'honorary black' following Alison Heisch's phrase 'honorary male' in relation to Elizabeth I. Heisch, in her essay, 'Queen Elizabeth I and the persistence of patriarchy', argues that Elizabeth strengthened patriarchal rule by emphasising her masculine attributes; I am suggesting that Othello stresses his usefulness to white society, his adoption of its rules of conduct, his achievements, which make him acceptable in order to efface the negative connotations of blackness, in the same way that Elizabeth needed to claim that she had a heart and stomach of a king even though she had the body of a woman.

Prejudice at Once Fulfilled and Rejected in *Othello*

Karen Newman

Karen Newman, a professor of comparative literature at Brown University, is the author of several books, including Fashioning Femininity and English Renaissance Drama.

In the following excerpt, Newman maintains that the white males who constitute Venice's power structure feel threatened by what they view as a dangerous, oversexed black male, a view represented by Iago, who has the attention, not only of the other white males in the play, but also the audience. To undermine his rival Othello and Othello's marriage, Iago repeats the theory that the black man will corrupt the white woman and their descendents. Despite the whites' desire to exclude and escape the contagion of the black race, Desdemona is ravenous for knowledge of what is different, eagerly asking Othello for tales of his exotic adventures. But, unlike Desdemona, Othello is duped by the racist Iago and, through his distrust, fulfills the prejudiced view of him. Still, William Shakespeare counters his own culture's attitudes by making a black man the tragic hero of his play and Desdemona's love for him genuine.

For the white male characters of [*Othello*], the black man's power resides in his sexual difference from a white male norm.

Iago Represents the White Male Fear of Black Sexuality

Their preoccupation with black sexuality is not an eruption of a normally repressed animal sexuality in the 'civilized' white male, but of the feared power and potency of a different and monstrous sexuality which threatens the white male sexual norm represented in the play most emphatically by Iago. For however evil Iago reveals himself to be . . . , Iago enjoys a privileged relation with the audience. He possesses what can be termed the discourse of knowledge in *Othello* and annexes not only the other characters, but the resisting spectator as well, into his world and its perspective. By virtue of his manipulative power and his superior knowledge and control over the action, which we share, we are implicated in his machinations and the cultural values they imply. . . .

Before the English had wide experience of miscegenation, they seem to have believed . . . that the black man had the power to subjugate his partner's whiteness, to make both his 'victim' and her offspring resemble him, to make them both black, a literal blackness in the case of a child, a metaphorical blackness in the case of a sexual partner. So in *Othello*, Desdemona becomes 'thou black weed' (IV iii 69) and the white pages of her 'goodly book' are blackened by writing when Othello imagines 'whore' inscribed across them. At IV iii, she explicitly identifies herself with her mother's maid Barbary whose name connotes blackness. The union of Desdemona and Othello represents a sympathetic identification between femininity and the monstrous. . . .

Desdemona Is Hungry for Difference

But Desdemona *hears* Othello and loves him, awed by his traveller's tales of the dangers he had passed, dangers which emphasize his link with monsters and marvels. Her responses to his tales are perceived as voracious—she 'devours' his discourses with a 'greedy ear'. . . .

When Desdemona comes to tell her version of their wooing, she says: 'I saw Othello's visage in his mind.' The allusion here is certainly to her audience's prejudice against the black 'visage' that both the [Venetian] Senators and Shakespeare's audience see in Othello, but Desdemona 'saw' his visage through hearing the tales he tells of his past, tales which, far from washing the Moor white as her line seems to imply, emphatically affirm Othello's link with Africa and its legendary monstrous creatures.

Othello Fulfils Cultural Prejudices

[Seventeenth-century English historian Thomas] Rymer's moral points up the patriarchal and scopic assumptions of his culture which are assumed as well in the play and most pointedly summoned up by Brabantio's often quoted lines: 'Look to her, Moor, have a quick eye to see: / She has deceiv'd her father, may do thee' (I iii 292–3). Fathers have the right to dispose of their daughters as they see fit, to whom they see fit, and disobedience against the father's law is merely a prelude to the descent into hell and blackness the play enacts, a fall, we might recall. . . .

The irony, of course, is that Othello himself is the instrument of punishment; he enacts the moral Rymer and Cinthio point [to], both confirming cultural prejudice by his monstrous murder of Desdemona and punishing her desire which transgresses the norms of the Elizabethan sex/race system. Both Othello and Desdemona deviate from the norms of the sex/race system in which they participate from the margins. Othello is not, in Cinthio's words, 'da noi,' one of 'us,' nor is Desdemona. Women depend for the class status on their affiliation with men—fathers, husbands, sons—and Desdemona forfeits that status and the protection it affords when she marries outside the categories her culture allows. For her transgression, her desire of difference, she is punished not only in a loss of status, but even of life. The woman's desire is punished, and ultimately its monstrous inspiration as well. As the object of Desdemona's illegitimate passion, Othello both figures monstrosity *and* at the same time represents the white male norms the play encodes through Iago, Roderigo, Brabantio. Not surprisingly, Othello reveals at last a complicitous self-loathing, for blackness is . . . loathsome to him. . . .

The aptly and ironically named Bianca is a cypher for Desdemona whose 'blackened whiteness' she embodies. Plots of desire conventionally figure woman as the erotic object, but in *Othello* the iconic centre of the spectacle is shifted from the woman to the monstrous Othello whose blackness charms *and* threatens, but ultimately fulfils the cultural prejudices it represents. Othello is both hero and outsider because he embodies not only the norms of male power and privilege represented by the white male hegemony which rules Venice, a world of prejudice, ambition, jealousy, and the denial of difference, but also the threatening power of the alien; Othello is a monster in the Renaissance sense of the word, a deformed creature like the hermaphrodites and other strange spectacles which so fascinated the early modern period. . . .

Shakespeare was certainly subject to the racist, sexist, and colonialist discourses of his time, but by making the black Othello a hero, and by making Desdemona's love for Othello, and her transgression of her society's norms for women in choosing him, sympathetic, Shakespeare's play stands in a contestatory relation to the . . . ideologies of race and gender in early modern England. Othello is, of course, the play's hero only within the terms of a white, elitist male ethos, and he suffers the generic 'punishment' of tragedy, but he is nevertheless represented as heroic and tragic at a historical moment when the only role blacks played on stage was that of a villain of low status.

Racism Is Not a Key Element in *Othello*

Meredith Anne Skura

Meredith Anne Skura, the Libby Shearn Moody Professor of English at Rice University, is the author of The Literary Use of the Psychoanalytic Process, Tudor Autobiography, and Shakespeare the Actor.

The question of whether a black man can be a hero or whether William Shakespeare presented a racist point of view in Othello *have been important arguments among leading critics. In this essay, Skura argues that Shakespeare's departure from typical Elizabethan texts shows that* Othello *is not a racist play. When black characters first appeared in English literature and history, they were not ethnically inferior and were seen as allies of England in the war against Spain. Nor were blacks and Moors in London seen as disruptive or demon-like. Nonjudgmental accounts of black men marrying white women appeared in the records. There is racial prejudice on the part of characters in* Othello, *but Othello is not stereotyped. Contrasting* Othello *with Shakespeare's source for the story, the Italian novelist Cinthio, shows, in the details Shakespeare changed, that he did not intend Othello's weaknesses to come from his ethnicity. Instead, Othello is presented as a universal hero, subject to the passions common to all people.*

Othello has become a play about its hero's blackness, and, for many, a racist play. Until the nineteenth century, the Moor was a tragic hero whose color was irrelevant and whose greatness and savagery could be considered together without contradiction. Once his color became important, that union was no longer possible.

Meredith Anne Skura, "Reading Othello's Skin: Contexts and Pretexts," *Philological Quarterly*, vol. 87, Summer 2008, pp. 299–334. Copyright © 2008 by *Philological Quarterly*. All rights reserved. Reproduced by permission.

Whether a Black Man Can Be a Hero

Some critics argued that Othello is a great hero and therefore he could not be black, but others argued that he regresses to primitive blackness and therefore could not be a true hero. Both judgments were born of empire. A similar attitude had already been mocked in E.M. Forster's 1924 *Passage to India*, when, despite appearances, an Anglo-Indian (wrongly) suspects Aziz of attacking the heroine simply because that's what Indians are really like once you get to know them. Martin Orkin's 1986 essay ["*Othello* and the 'Plain Face' of Racism," *Shakespeare Quarterly*, vol. 38, 1987] incisively analyzed the covert racist assumptions on which such opinions are based. Nonetheless the opinion has prevailed, although it is now attributed to Shakespeare, not the critics. As Laurence Lerner put it [as quoted by Orkin], "Shakespeare suffered from colour prejudice."

The play has since been read in the context of discourse about color prejudice in our world as well as Shakespeare's. It has been seen in terms of Anglo American experience with sub-Saharan Africans, whether in the United States (Richard Wright's *Native Son*, Ralph Ellison's *Invisible Man*), or South Africa (Janet Suzman's *Othello*), or, more recently, in postcolonialism everywhere. . . . Rewritings of Othello are now regularly incorporated in the study of the original play.

The Racial Context in Which Shakespeare Wrote

The following discussion tries instead to understand what *Othello* might have meant to Shakespeare. . . . My assumption, however is that understanding the play first in its own terms is the best way to understand its role in history, and in what follows I deal only with material roughly contemporary with it that has left a mark on the play. There certainly was an extensive discourse about black people and Moors available to Shakespeare, much of it racist or proto-racist by today's standards. But the odd thing is that *Othello* in fact echoes so little from these potential sources or pretexts. Shakespeare ignores many of them, parodies others, omits racist sections of texts he used, and turns instead to a surprising number of other texts seldom or never mentioned in contemporary debates about race. The argument below contradicts recent claims about *Othello*'s racism. It first sets out the assumptions, definitions, pretexts, and evidence on which the argument rests, and then goes on to focus on Shakespeare's revisions of *Othello*'s most important proto-racist pretext. . . .

Richard Hakluyt, perhaps the most proto-imperialist of the Elizabethans, collected reports of their adventures in his early anthologies, hoping to encourage more Englishmen to explore and claim new lands that were still open for exploitation. The descriptions in Hakluyt varied widely from admiration to disgust, from seeming objectivity to outrageous fantasy, and some of them, like the lines about skin color in George Best's 1578 *True Discourse of his Northwest voyages*, are Proto-racist. As [critic] Greg Bak has argued, this subsection of *Othello*'s larger context supplies most of the evidence for claims about the play's racism. . . .

Many, though not all, in Shakespeare's authence could distinguish the North African "Moors" with varied physical characteristics from the less familiar "Africans" or "Negroes," thought to have dark skin, thick lips and woolly hair. Leo Africanus's *Historie and Geographie of Africa*, the period's authoritative history and geography of Africa, describes Morocco as "a noble site," one of the greatest "in the whole world," and for the English, it was an entity like France or Spain, as were Fez and other Barbary states. North Africa was a locus of rich and powerful peoples close to the heart of civilization; they were seen as formidable enemies, or, increasingly, potential allies and trading partners, but certainly not ignorant, amoral monsters. Medieval Christians saw the Islamic world as its demonic Other, but as English experience with Mediterranean traffic increased, statesmen and merchants alike began to re-think the old stereotype more pragmatically. Unlike the adventurers, however, they did so in terms of religion, not skin color or other "black" behavior. To win support for an alliance with Morocco, for example, Edmund Hogan, a London mercer, emphasized the similarity between Islam and Protestantism, while to protest an alliance John de Cardenas described Muslims as heathens defying Christianity.

Blackness and Moors in Elizabethan Drama

Certainly for Elizabethan drama the Mediterranean discourse was more important than New World or sub-Saharan reports. All the black "Africans" in the period's plays come from Morocco or Fez, as does [the prince of] Morocco in *Merchant of Venice*. Christopher Marlowe's early Moors, like Robert Greene's in *Selimus and Alphonsus*, were enemies of the Christians but not sub-Saharan. Not that they were tawny—most likely they were black . . . but blackness made them geographically exotic, not ethnically inferior. Muley Mahamet in George Peele's *Battle of Alcazar* (1588), the first of the villainous black Moors, was also defined by this Eastern world, not the "Africa" that lay south; but his color symbolized evil, and, like the devils accompanying Mahamet on stage, it distinguished him from his virtuous also Moorish half-brother, the rightful prince. Peele rationalized Mahamet's difference by assigning him a "Negro" mother who no more represents actual Negroes than the evil mothers of Cloten in *Pericles* or Caliban in *The Tempest* represent actual British or Algerians. Nonetheless, her presence introduced the possibility of an ethnic as well as symbolic meaning for blackness that would be exploited in later Moors, but not yet.

Meanwhile, drama in this period was also affected by the fact that historical Moors, unlike Turks, were potential allies against the Spanish. A possible alliance was discussed when the Moroccan ambassadors made their much remarked upon visit to London in 1601. [Literary scholar] Barbara Everett suggested long ago that critics move Othello out of Africa and into the Mediterranean world. The opening antagonism in Othello between the Moor on one side, and Iago, named after the Moor-killing Spanish St. James, and Spanish-sounding "Roderigo" on the other, is less a reference to anything English than to the well known Spanish antagonism to Moors. Prince Eleazar of Fez and Barbary, in Thomas Decker's *Lust's Dominion* (1600?), brought back by King Philip as war prisoner, is similarly vilified by the Spanish court, but the Spaniards are as bad as he is.

Apparently Little Racism in England

A third important context for Othello has remained largely untapped by arguments for racism. This is Londoners' very different experience of the resident strangers, identified variously as Mores, Negroes, Indians, and Guineans in the parish registers, law courts, inventory and payment lists. Imtiaz Habib identifies records for about 100 Londoners from Elizabeth's coronation in 1558 until Othello was performed (c. 1605) who were or may have been Moors or Africans. Most of these had ties to Spain or Portugal, although they had most probably come from the Americas, Africa, and the Indies. They were neither wealthy officials like the Moroccan ambassadors nor sinister figures like Muly Mahamet. Many were bond-slaves, servants living with their masters, or prostitutes, but some were ordinary workers, skilled musicians, or craftsmen with valuable trade secrets, even, possibly, brothel keepers. They lived in neighborhoods at the east and west ends of London where other foreigners had settled. Their presence, their baptisms, and their church attendance were taken for granted and recorded without remark, as was Mrs. Peirs's visit to Doctor Simon Forman with her twelve-year-old "blackmor" maid, Polonia, because Polonia had pain in her stomach, fever, and a "faint harte". The records reveal no arrests or conflicts, although a Portuguese in London complained that although his newly purchased Ethiopian servant refused to serve him, he had no remedy in English law.

Interracial Marriages in London

Previous scholarship has noted the presence of black people in London but has barely begun to explore their significance for early modern attitudes. For example, important information has been overlooked even in the passage in Best's "True Discourse" so often cited as evidence for English xenophobia:

> I myself have seen an Ethiopean as black as a coal brought into England, who, taking a fair English woman to Wife, begat a son in all respects as black as the father was, although England were his native Country, and an English woman his Mother: whereby it seemeth this blackness proceedeth rather of some natural infection of that man ... and therefore we cannot impute it to the nature of the Clime.

The casual way Best mentions marriage between black and white is as informative as his thoughts about "infection," and it corroborates the records now being uncovered about surprising numbers of interracial marriages.

Othello looks different when seen in the larger context of England's many different relationships to Moors, Africans, and other people of color—especially those at home—rather than only the most racist of them. . . .

Shakespeare Never Racist in *Othello*

Othello's color, . . . does not explain his savagery. Only Emilia comes close to saying so when she finds Desdemona and spits out insults about a black "devil." But her racism is contradicted by what follows, as Iago's slurs were contradicted before, this time by Othello's repentance and suicide, and Othello's blackness remains irrelevant to everyone else on stage. Perhaps the reason that arguments for Othello's racism so often evoke external stereotypes is that there is nothing so definitive in the play itself. No one calls Othello "slave of Barbary," ..., and no one ever says that he lapses into being a hot African, or a Moor, or even a literally, rather than figuratively, black man. They are shocked because they never thought that he, of all people, was capable of such behavior. At the end, even Cassio, Othello's innocent victim, calls him "great of heart" (5.2.359). Othello's last words show that he kills himself because he has newly turned Turk, not because he has lapsed back into being a stereotype of anything.

The lack of explicit stereotyping in the text is more obvious when it is compared to the pretext [storyline] that *Othello* follows most closely, Giraldi Cinthio's novella about a Moorish Captain and his wife.... Cinthio includes an explicitly racist stereotype called up by "Desdemona" herself. Terrified when the Moor turns jealous, she reverts to cliched thinking: "You Moors are so hot by nature that any little thing moves you to anger and revenge." Elsewhere she says she should never have disobeyed her parents to marry someone so unlike herself. But Desdemona's corresponding line in Othello is quite different: "And yet I fear you, for you're fatal then / When your eyes roll so" (5.2.37–39). Cinthio's Desdemona sees a stereotypical Moor, but Desdemona sees Othello in a frighteningly passionate and jealous mood. Ignoring the color of his skin, she refers to his rolling eyes. A reader today might take rolling eyes to indicate his stereotypical blackness. But for Shakespeare, rolling eyes signaled passion, whether in whites or blacks, men or women. In particular they signaled the passion of jealousy, the play's explanation for Othello's behavior....

Othello's Blackness Not Responsible for the Murder

Othello's jealousy, not his blackness or his Moorish origin, is responsible for the murder. Jealousy, the "green-eyed monster" (3.3.168, 3.4.161) is the only monster in this play, apart from the tempest's "monstrous" surges (2.1.13), the natural world's analogy to jealousy. Of the nine other appearances of "monster" or "monstrous" in *Othello*, none is connected with blackness. Three refer to the "monster" in Iago's thought, to the monstrous fantasies plucked from it when his invention gives birth (1.3.403, 3.3.107), and to the "monstrous" act they lead him to (5.2.187). Iago's self-engendered monster, erupts from his brain into Othello's head and makes the Moor think "adulterous" Desdemona is monstrous (3.3.428) and that "a horned man's a monster" (4.1.63).

Degrading stereotypes of blacks and Moors were part of Shakespeare's world. But, again, the question is whether any of them affected the play. . . .

Shakespeare's Changes to His Model Shows His Rejection of Stereotypes

Shakespeare borrowed more *Othello*-material from Cinthio's novella than from than any other pretext. Oddly, although it can be seen as a proto-racist document, Cinthio is mentioned only in passing or not a all in claims about *Othello*'s racism, and never in claims about stereotypes. Yet *Othello*'s difference from Cinthio provides some of the best evidence we have for its relation to its proto-racist context. . . .

Different as the two texts are in their accounts of the Moor's temptation, Shakespeare's most remarkable change affects everything that follows it. In Cinthio, once the Moor is jealous, he becomes a ruthless monster, savage but cunning. He devises a murder that Aaron [the Moor in Shakespeare's *Titus Andronicus*] might admire. He and the Ensign beat Disdemona to death with a sockful of sand and bury her under fallen lumber to conceal their act. Although the Moor misses his wife afterward, he never admits his guilt (blaming it all on the Ensign), never repents, and hides from retribution. He loses all connection to the rational, "gallant Moor" he was at first and never regains it. The tale degenerates into a sordid scrabble for revenge among the Ensign, the Moor, and Disdemona's family.

By the fourth act *Othello* leaves all traces of Cinthio behind. It's not that *Othello* downplays the savagery of the murder itself. *Othello*'s brutality is more intimate and emotional than Cinthio's, and its interracial physicality unlike anything staged in earlier drama. But while the murder is more disturbing than Cinthio's, it is less purely the result of Othello's ethnicity. Cinthio's protagonist murdered his wife because he was a vengeful hot Moor. Othello murders because he loves his wife too much. Unlike Cinthio's Moor, Othello recovers from his madness, judges it [harshly] . . . and punishes himself. His behavior at the end is also unlike anything in earlier Moors. Instead it recalls other famous love-murders in European and classical tradition. Cinthio's Moor was an isolated exception in European life; Shakespeare weaves Othello into the fabric of European culture. . . .

Othello's Crimes Are Not Race Related

Othello's crime is monstrous, but Shakespeare does not allow his . . . [audience] the comfort of thinking that he is capable of monstrosity because he is a Moor. He is one of us, not one of them. His repentance may come too late; it can neither undo what he did nor save him. But it universalizes his passion and moves it toward heroic or tragic stature, as well as toward the sad common denominator of human comedy. The several pretexts discussed here—no doubt along with others no longer available to us—weave Shakespeare's Moor seamlessly into the texture of Western narratives about destructive passion, making his connection to Moors far less important than in the story of Cinthio's Moor and than it is to us. Response to Cinthio's anecdote was more black and white. . . .

Proto-racist discourse was circulating when Shakespeare wrote and affected his most important pretext in Cinthio, but he seems to have ignored much of it. He de-emphasized racial difference in Cinthio's story and, with his new ending he finally defeated expectations about stereotypical black Moors.

Parts of Othello that readers have found provocatively similar to proto-racist discourse elsewhere seem less so once the rest of Othello's discursive and historical context is taken into account. . . .

This is not to ignore other operative prejudices at work in the play—against Turks for example, or drunken Danes, Germans and "swag-bellied" Hollanders (2.3.73,74)—or to argue for Shakespeare's moral superiority. He was not the first to question stereotypes. . . . Of course racial difference matters in Othello, but as in Shakespeare's other work, the play's emphasis is on interrogating mindless, rigid belief like Titus Andronicus's Roman piety or Brabantio's proto-racism. As [critic] George Hunter argued at the beginning of debate over Othello's color, the entire play is structured to raise and defeat mindless expectation about many things—not only black Moors but also Turkish attack, a comic ending, loose women, plain blunt soldiers, and so on. . . . However, the text includes little or no evidence for the structural production of today's racism. This is a play about prejudice, not race, which is why Iago is more important than Cinthio's Ensign. . . .

The search in *Othello* for ever less blatant forms of racism can be valuable for us today, but the approach seems particularly inappropriate to this play. *Othello* is, after all, about a great man whose tragedy lies in his insistent romantic belief that the world is wholly good, that his "perfect soul" will protect him from prejudice, and that Iago could not possibly be dishonest. Yet even he sees, too late, that a devil like Iago can never be killed, only acknowledged. To believe today that if one only tries hard enough Iago can be overcome—that a text can be made completely free of prejudice for imperfect, human audiences—is to start the tragedy all over again.

Othello's Marriage to Desdemona Incites Racism

Lara Bovilsky

Lara Bovilsky, a professor of English at the University of Oregon, has written on race in Renaissance drama.

In the following excerpt Bovilsky notes that before his marriage, Othello is regarded as a skilled warrior and diplomat, and race is not an issue. Race only becomes an issue when he marries a white woman, after which Othello is caught in an explosion of racial hatred, initiated by Iago. Othello's marriage to a white Venetian causes him to be viewed as a filthy animal with the capability of infecting Desdemona. Desdemona's father, inflamed by Iago, becomes outraged at the prospect of having mixed-race grandchildren and, further, fears that his descendants will pollute the state itself.

Waiting for Othello to arrive at the Cyprian harbor, Iago and Desdemona pass the time by trading bawdy quips. In rhymed couplets provoking appreciative groans from Desdemona, Iago serially pokes fun at wise and foolish, "fair" and "black" women. According to Iago, all these women scheme for sexual encounters. . . . Iago's generalizing couplets draw attention to pairings of complexion and sexuality. . . . Iago uses "black" to signify both female darkness and female promiscuity:

If she be black, and thereto have a wit,

She'll find a white that shall her blackness fit. (2.1.132–33)

Iago's pun on "white"/"wight" (man) implies the sexual nature of female blackness. More obviously, his couplet suggests the inevitability of a miscegenistic sexuality, that whiteness and blackness "fit." This "fit" echoes the logic of Desdemona's marriage. . . .

Iago: "Fairness" in Women Is Easily Blackened

Iago's couplet suggests that female wit uses fairness so that fairness may be used sexually. As we will see, such uses of fairness are imagined as damaging and, through the Renaissance association of promiscuity with blackness, darkening to fairness. Iago here imagines that female fairness is intended to be damaged in this way ("for use"), setting out, witty or foolish, to undo itself. . . .

All too predictably, Desdemona's eager participation in Iago's rhetorical game has proved disturbing to the play's readers: the interchange is omitted in every production of which I am aware, and critical opinion has been overwhelmingly negative. Epitomizing the negative view, M.R. Ridley notes:

> This is to many readers, and I think rightly, one of the most unsatisfactory passages in Shakespeare. To begin with it is unnatural . . . then, it is distasteful to watch her engaged in a long piece of cheap backchat with Iago, and so adept at it that one wonders how much time on the voyage was spent in the same way.

Ridley's concerns about Desdemona's "adeptness" at "cheap" repartee all too quickly set him on a jealous train of thought, wondering, like Othello, what she does when she's not in front of him and echoing Iago's conclusions about the prurient ambitions of the dangerous female combination of "fairness and wit" (2.1.129). Critics worry that Desdemona's racy joking with Iago undercuts viewer/reader sympathy for her, as she must be utterly "innocent" for her murder to fully outrage the audience (as her servant Emilia's hardly ever does). She must have no whisper of extramural sexual experience, which the Renaissance sometimes called "blackness" about her.

Racial Blackness and Moral Blackness

Early modern moralizing on chastity may seem a strange place to look for prevailing racialist doctrine. The equation between figurative darkening and the transgression of female chastity may be so familiar to the reader of Shakespeare as to pass without comment. After all, female "blackness" is metaphorical; although critics have noted the terminological overlap, Desdemona's "blackness" and Othello's "blackness" have generally been regarded as two quite different phenomena. . . .

Desdemona Blackened by Her Marriage

From its very first scene, *Othello* is saturated with the imagery and concerns that make it the most familiar example of an English Renaissance play interested and invested in race. In that scene, in dialogue with Roderigo and Desdemona's father, Brabantio, Iago employs varied elements of an apparently vast manipulative repertoire of racist barbs, innuendo, stereotypes, and threats. Combining these, Iago presents ideas about Desdemona's and Othello's marriage as a mixture of kinds whose participants possess a disturbing animality; he hints at an accompanying inheritance of undesirable traits. His depictions rely on additional ideologies of gender, nation, religion, and a materialist understanding of familial integrity for their application to Othello and Desdemona. In response, Roderigo and Brabantio are quick to make their own contributions, referring to Othello in language that insults his appearance and interprets his behavior as reflecting malign alien origins. As we will see, they refer to Desdemona in similarly charged racial language, describing her as physically compromised by her alliance and as compromising Brabantio as well, through her betrayal of their shared "blood."

Collectively, then, this scene presents racial content of nearly every kind. . . . Strikingly, even the racial insults that most exaggerate Othello's perceived racial difference—those that compare him to animals—are applied to him mainly in the context of his relationship with Desdemona. . . . Iago's famous lines, "even now, now, very now, an old black ram / Is tupping your white ewe" (1.1.87–88), exemplify such bestial imagery. Intending to outrage Brabantio, Iago arranges a set of recognizable antitheticals (black/white, ram/ewe) that heighten a perceived opposition between Othello and Desdemona in order to dramatize its breach. . . .

If Othello is compared to an animal, Iago's antithesis figures Desdemona as one of the same kind, a sameness that complicates her status as someone imperiled by the threat of exogamy [marrying outside one's social group]. Rather, because ram and ewe are an antithesis properly matched, Iago's image can imply a likeness between Desdemona and Othello revealed by their matched bestial labels and sexual compatibility. . . .

Othello's Race an Issue Only After His Marriage

Outside of the context of his relation to Desdemona, language demeaning Othello or even emphasizing him as a racialized subject is initially absent. The senate is chiefly occupied with the threat posed by "the Turk," who, as the "general enemy" (1.3.49) with an alien religion, culture, and competing imperialism, monopolizes senatorial defensive and xenophobic energies. The Duke and senators are sufficiently invested in Othello to send three parties searching for him (1.2.46), and the Duke greets "valiant Othello" before Senator Brabantio (1.3.49) when the two enter the council chamber together, though the presence of both has been remarked (1.3.48). Sent to Cyprus, Othello replaces the governor, Montano, whose experiences with Othello do not dispose him to resent the dispossession.

Rather, Montano exhibits relief: "I am glad on't, 'tis a worthy governor ... for I have served him, and the man commands like a full soldier", (2.1.30, 35–36) and, like the senators, unlike Iago or Roderigo, calls his governor by name: "brave Othello" (2.1.38).

Othello's praise echoes through the first two acts—at least, his praise by those involved with him through state business. This praise has often been taken as exposition meant to highlight the pathos of Othello's decline into slavish and irrational murderousness, but it can also be seen as demarking an unproblematic context for Othello's presence in Venetian society, a zone in which racial differences are irrelevant, to be compared with the racialized hostility attending Othello's marriage that is also present from the beginning. The contrast is most spectacularly seen in Brabantio, who invited Othello over "oft" before the marriage (1.3.129), presumably to curry favor with the senate's rising military star, but who is sufficiently outraged by Othello's marriage to spew a litany of accusations that center on Othello's foreignness and the disruption of Venetian bloodlines. Likewise, Othello's status as rival to Roderigo, and, later, Roderigo's wishful and projective thinking about Othello as a cuckold and rejected lover, are produced by Othello's relation to Desdemona; it is Othello's connection to Desdemona that unleashes in Roderigo the string of physical slurs and inappropriately familiar speech that mark Othello as a racialized outsider. As a result, the racial tension experienced around Othello is generated by his union with Desdemona, not only in the compressed racial logics of Iago's vicious attacks (which are, in fact, echoed by these other characters) but also through the tensions of more dilated social narrative. . . .

Depiction of Interracial Unions

Erotic interracial relationships are readily, in fact frequently, thematized in English Renaissance texts—so much so, that their proliferation would seem to satisfy a deeper desire for and pleasure in the ostensibly disturbing representations of miscegenation themselves. Miscegenation provides extensive material for Shakespeare. Iago's representation of sexuality and gender difference as a matrix of race provides one theoretically important instance and explanation for this extensive use. As topic and trope, miscegenation's figuration may reach an apotheosis [exaltation] in its fantastic amplification in *Othello*, but it is repeatedly used elsewhere, from Aaron's sexual involvement with Tamora in *Titus Andronicus*, to Antony's with Cleopatra in *Antony and Cleopatra* to Claribel's wedding in Tunis in *The Tempest*. . . .

Desdemona Already "Blackened" by Her Refusal of White Suitors

By the end of the seventeenth century, Thomas Rymer, in [Karen] Newman's words, "a kind of critical Iago," was able to generalize on the topic, reading *Othello* as "a caution to all Maidens of Quality how, without their parents consent, they run away with Blackamoors." Rymer's warning is pointedly directed at the female member of the couple, who is assumed to be both fairer and richer than the "blackamoor" she is so drawn to when unhindered by parental controls. As we will see, such an elopement carries a price. While one may object to an argument that employs Rymer as a representative reader of *Othello* (his book presents a rabid critique of the play), his interpretation is indeed anticipated by Iago, who contrasts the fact that Desdemona consents to miscegenate with her earlier resistance to desirable matches, in order to suggest to Othello her inevitable errancy:

> Not to affect many proposed matches
>
> Of her own clime, complexion and degree,
>
> Whereto we see, in all things, nature tends—
>
> Foh! one may smell in such a will most rank,
>
> Foul disproportion, thoughts unnatural. (3.3.233–37). . .

The Fear of Othello's Potential Offspring Is Racially Charged

Iago's insinuations that Desdemona's extreme gentleness is itself a precursor to miscegenation and promiscuity attest to the way in which Desdemona's chastity and her marriage to Othello raise racial anxieties that dog both characters. . . . But to assess the play's total range of such anxieties, it is important to note that the causes and results of the interracial marriage are not imputed to Desdemona's psychology alone, nor are the repercussions of the marriage confined to her "sacrifice" (5.2.65) at the altar of Othello's jealousy. Iago's racial ideology is invested in pathologizing Othello and his descendants as well, often independently of Desdemona. When Iago threatens Brabantio that "the devil will make a grandsire of you" (1.1.90), he appeals to medieval traditions of religious iconography that represented devils with black skin. Significantly, however, Iago links this reference to a threat of inherited blackness that will reflect back on Brabantio through his "blood" connection to his grandchild, that is, to an ideology of genealogical relation that is not simply theological. Iago's threat reveals the use to which religious color iconographies can be put, for even if one were to argue that the representation of devils in blackface need not be racist, Iago's link of such representations to genealogy shows that they may be made to signify in a highly racialist and racist way. . . .

Pointedly, in the image emphasizing the genealogical threat, unlike the image of ram and ewe, Othello's sexuality is imagined as less than human in contrast to Desdemona's: "you'll have your daughter covered with a Barbary horse; you'll have your nephews neigh to you, you'll have coursers for cousins and jennets for germans!" (1.1.109–12). Brabantio's daughter's elopement is imagined as immediately and almost parodically fertile, surrounding its patriarch with an alien, preverbal clan, derided as not even belonging to the same species as Brabantio. . . .

Othello and Desdemona, played by Eamonn Walker and Zoe Tapper, share a kiss in a 2007 production of Othello *at Shakespeare's Globe Theatre in London.* © Elliott Franks/ WireImage.

Whichever the domains of Venetian privilege and group identity being made vulnerable, however, the mechanism of the threat is a racial one: Brabantio, assuming that Othello is pagan and slave material, claims that these qualities will be disseminated throughout Venice, inherited by Othello's off- spring. It is important to note that Brabantio imagines broad politically apocalyptic repercussions from the match between Othello and Desdemona, and these repercussions are declared to result specifically from offspring that will, unavoidably it seems, be tainted by Othello's racial legacy. . . .

At times, then, Othello's race is represented as dominant and menacing, constituting an external threat to the Venetian polity itself. His status as racial and national outsider—a "wheeling stranger" or "erring Barbarian" (1.1.134, 1.3.356)— with an exotic past is seen as static and unassimilable in Venice. This is precisely the view expressed in Brabantio's characterization of Othello's genealogical threat to Venetian "statesmen," a view that depends upon erasing Desdemona's role in contributing to that legacy or, for that matter, in pursuing Othello as husband (and so finding him assimilable). . . .

Lack of Female Virtue Is Tied to Racial Darkness

The indictment of female virtue is definitively tied to racist imagery of moral darkness. Othello's image of Desdemona's moral and racial pollution trades on these associations in endorsing Iago's and Brabantio's reasoning: Desdemona was chastest and also whitest when she refused all marriages proposed to her. Her shamefast blushes, masking sexual response, figured forth the racial darkening that was her fate as soon as she agreed to marry.

As we saw with Iago's joking couplets, female sexual behavior is often characterized in this way as darkness or . . . as darkening or dirtying. . . .

Iago notes the role of slander and malice in effecting such transformations, when he emblematizes them: "I'll pour this pestilence into his ear . . . So will I turn her virtue into pitch" [tar] (2.3.351, 355). Iago imagines both his poisonously persuasive force and Desdemona's corrupted virtue as actual fluid substances, and virtue in particular, once "fair" and possessed of all "delighted beauty" (1.3.290), has become dark, warm, and viscous "pitch." . . .

Interestingly, the racialized associations of marriage and adultery that accrue to her do not require that Othello be racially different from her, but these associations are occasionally intensified with remarks about Othello's background or appearance, remarks seemingly generated for that purpose alone. The descriptions of Desdemona's racial transformation reference both her alleged adultery and her willful marriage, suggesting that both licit and illicit forms of female sexuality are sufficient to precipitate racial degeneration.

Attitudes About Race Shift in *Othello*

Emma Smith

Emma Smith, a prolific Shakespearean scholar, is a lecturer at Oxford University.

In the following excerpt, Smith points out that ideas of racial differences shift within in Othello, which serves to highlight issues of alienation and belonging. The play has proved relevant to contemporary issues about race unknown in William Shakespeare's time, including apartheid in South Africa and legal racial segregation was in the United States. Arguments continue about Othello's color. Several Elizabethan events may have been on Shakespeare's mind. Although Elizabethans associated "blackamoors" with devilish sexuality, in Shakespeare's Othello it is the racist Iago who is given these characteristics of sexual obsession and alienation. Repeatedly Shakespeare "turned the tables on our racist expectations," Smith argues. Only at the end of the play does Othello lapse into stereotype. He becomes a black outsider whose property (Desdemona) is being threatened.

Why does Othello, in that final speech, shift the question of racial otherness into the multifarious exoticism of Aleppo, the 'turbaned Turk', 'Arabian trees', 'base Indian' (5.2.356–62)—or, as some texts modernize the Folio's 'Iudean', 'Judean'—all the while ignoring the identity of 'Moor' with which the play labels him from its title onwards? Shifting ideas of racial difference are a crucial—and problematic—aspect of the play and of its reception. When American literature professor Emily Bartels notes that her students, on reading *Othello*, always want to talk about race, she implies that

Emma Smith, "Race and *Othello*," *William Shakespeare: Othello*, Devon, UK: Northcote House Publishers Ltd., 2005, pp. 24–48. Copyright © 2005 by Northcote House Publishers Ltd. All rights reserved. Reproduced by permission.

this 'so often tend[s] to simplify the story'. Rather it seems to me to complicate it in ways that force us to acknowledge similarities and differences between our own perspectives and those of early modern audiences, which bring us up against notions of prejudice that cannot be comfortably consigned to history, and that implicate us in the racially configured discourses out of which the play was written and in which it has continued to be read and performed.

Race, Alienation, and Belonging

Far from simplifying *Othello* and Othello, questions of race engage us in complex narratives of belonging and alienation. *Othello* has shaped racial understanding in a range of ways unthinkable to Shakespeare and his original audiences: as the novelist Ben Okri has observed, if it 'is not a play about race, then its history has made it one'. . . . When Janet Suzman produced the play in the Market Theatre of Johannesburg during apartheid, she and John Kani, who played Othello, were '*at last*, fired up after ten frustrating years of keeping a constant vigil for the play that might speak not just to both of us as actors but to our anguished country'; when the African-American actor Paul Robeson took on the role, he observed that Othello 'in the Venice of that time was in practically the same position as a coloured man in America today' both comments attest to the ongoing fact of the play's unsettling relevance. . . .

Othello and the Modern Audience

Perhaps it is even more dangerous to assume that we *should* attempt to separate our own racial blind spots and biases from those of the play. When, for example, scholars agonize over whether Shakespeare intended Othello as a tawny North African Arab—the literal associations of 'Moor' (first used at 1.1.39) and 'Barbary' (1.1.113)—or a black sub-Saharan African—Roderigo's slur 'thicklips' (1.1.66)—we may be justified in feeling that this is more a question about our own categories of racial difference than about those of the early Jacobean period. This sense of anachronism is heightened by the corollary of these arguments about Othello's provenance, which tends to suggest that the lighter his complexion, the more noble and tragic the character. Thus that *Othello* has always been about race is certain; that it has always been about the racial assumptions of its readers and audience members needs to be analysed as part of its ongoing tradition; that we cannot step outside its, and our, assumptions interpolates us as coadjutants in its compelling, terrifying mixture of racial fantasy.

A Possible Model for Othello

In [1596] Captain Caspar van Senden's request for a licence to deport 'blackmoors . . . into Spain and Portugal' was approved:

> Her Majesty . . . considereth . . . that those kind of people may be well spared in this realm, being so populous and numbers of able persons the subjects of the land and Christian people that perish for want of service, whereby through their labour they might be maintained. [You] are therefore required . . . to aid and assist him to take up such blackmoors as he shall find within this realm, with the consent of their masters, who we doubt not, considering her Majesty's good pleasure to have those kind of people sent out of the land . . . and that they shall do charitably and like Christians rather to be served by their own countrymen than with those kind of people, will yield those in their possession to him.

This licence was renewed five years later in 1601.

These documents identify black people as servants or slaves—'those in their possession'—but the second piece of relevant evidence associates Moors with nobility. The arrival of a courtly delegation from Barbary in North Africa in late 1600 caused a considerable stir in London. Led by the Moroccan ambassador Abdul El-Quahéd Ben Messasud, the emissaries were in England for six months, during which time Shakespeare's company, the Lord Chamberlain's Men, performed at court. An extant portrait of the ambassador shows an imperious figure wearing a pale turban, with a dark moustache and short beard, a hooked nose and a direct and piercing stare. His light-coloured garments are covered with a dark cloak and he wears an ornate sword. Looking at the portrait, Ernst Honigmann asks: 'Is it too fanciful to suppose that this very face haunted Shakespeare's imagination and inspired the writing of his tragedy?' It *is* certainly fanciful, but there is no doubt that the idea of Barbary reverberates throughout the play's verbal texture. Othello is called 'Barbary horse' (1.1.113–14) and 'erring barbarian' (1.3.354), and the word and some unexpected cognates recur visually and acoustically through the play, from Brabanzio, called Barbantio at several points in the stage directions and speech prefixes, the 'barbarous' brawl of 2.3.165, to the melancholy story of the maid called Barbary in 4.3.25–32.

Shakespeare inherited a black hero from the nameless Moor who is one of Cinthio's central protagonists. . . .

View of Blacks in England as Satanic and Sexually Predatory

Here, the socio-moral connotations of the Moor's race are not made explicit, and Cinthio's story stresses the extent to which his central protagonist is valued by the Venetian state. Audiences at the play's first performances, however, would have brought a host of associations, derived from a nexus of textual and material experiences, to the idea of a black character. Blackness was frequently associated with the devil and with wickedness: Reginald Scot, in his *The Discovery of Witchcraft* (1584), opined that 'a damned soul may and doth take the shape of a black moor' and in Samuel Harsnett's *A Declaration of Egregious Popish Impostures* (1603), known to have been read by Shakespeare, since he draws on it for names of devils in *King Lear*, a woman is tempted by a demon in the shape of 'a black man standing at the door and beckoning her to come away'. Thomas Heywood, in a play about travelling and English imperialism called *The Fair Maid of the West II* (1630), described 'a Moor/ Of all that bears man's shape likest a devil'. Emilia refers to this same tradition when she calls Othello 'the blacker devil' after the discovery of the murder of Desdemona, 'the more angel she' (5.2.140). Black characters on stage before *Othello* tended therefore to be villains, often clever, plotting and amoral, rather like *Titus Andronicus's* Aaron. In George Peele's *The Battle of Alcazar* (1598), the bombastic soldier Muly Hamet is described as 'black in his look, and bloody in his deeds', although he is flanked by an opposite 'brave barbarian lord Muly Molocco'. In (?) Thomas Dekker's *Lust's Dominion* (1600), Eleazar is a black character combining sexual transgression and machiavellian plotting. Even in a comedy, sexual predation of white women is seen as defining black masculinity. . . .

Many of the expectations evoked by the spectacle of a black character, therefore, were part of a long cultural tradition. This tradition was scarcely modified by the travellers' tales and exploration narratives that filled London's booksellers during the second half of the sixteenth century and beyond. . . .

Iago's Sexual Depravity

Sexual depravity and prowess were frequently associated with blackness in travel narratives, an association Roderigo articulates when he dubs Othello 'a lascivious Moor' (1.1.128). Leo Africanus, himself a converted Moor living in Italy, maintained that 'Negroes' 'have great swarms of harlots among them; whereupon a man may easily conjecture their manner of living' and that no people were 'more prone to venery' than the North African; other travellers discussed African tribes 'which like beasts live without wedding and dwell with women without law'. Surveying these narratives, Karen Newman concludes that 'always we find the link between blackness and the monstrous, and particularly a monstrous sexuality'; and Arthur Little concurs that *Othello* is working with and against existing stereotypes as a 'text that will at once unsettle and fill in, substantiate and resolve what the audience suspects it already knows about the essence of blackness as the savage and libidinous Other'.

Black characters were, therefore, already associated with stereotypical lust for sex and power. It could be argued that Shakespeare challenges these assumptions in *Othello*. Here he apparently splits the conventional black role into two, allocating its Machiavellian malignity to Iago, and its skin colour and sexuality to Othello. Many of the stereotypical attributes of blackness are thus identified with Iago: a man whose concept of sex is entirely physical; a plotter bent on revenge; the 'devil' (5.2.293) who cannot be killed at the end of the play. Whether or not Iago is explicitly racially motivated is difficult to judge, although his injunction to Cassio to drink 'the health of black Othello' (2.3.28–9) has more than a smack of racism. . . .

Reversing Stereotypes

Those characters in the play who articulate explicitly racist sentiments—Iago, Roderigo, Brabanzio—are not ones whose opinions or behaviour the play otherwise endorses, and it is surely significant that at no point in his relationship with Othello does the wronged Cassio ever play the race card. In more recent times, the play has not been entirely susceptible to a racially politicized reading. . . .

Desdemona's 'I saw Othello's visage in his mind' (1.3.252) suggests that her decision is in spite of his colour rather than because of it, although Robert Burton's *Anatomy of Melancholy* discusses, in his chapter on causes of love-melancholy,

Paul Robeson and Uta Hagen as Othello and Desdemona in a celebrated Broadway production of Othello, *1943. Robeson was the first black actor to perform the role of Othello with an all-white cast on the Broadway stage.* © AP Images.

that 'a black man is a pearl in a fair woman's eye' Laurence Olivier discussed the play's particular eroticism: 'it's tremendously, highly sexual because it's a black man', and this clearly has as much to tell us about the context of his interpretation as of the play itself. Arguably, Shakespeare seems to have turned the tables on racist expectations by showing us a black and a white character who have reversed the usual colour associations, performing the chromatic flip characteristic of the board game 'Othello'. Instead of the Moor as villain we have the Moor as hero.

There is a lot of truth in this vision of a play that challenges racial prejudices rather than endorsing them. . . . Thus the play is about racism and its effects; rather than being itself racist, it pursues an actively anti-racist agenda. This is an attractive view. We have so much invested in the idea of Shakespeare as a repository for liberal humanist values that it is disquieting to have to acknowledge that, on occasion, his plays fail to buttress contemporary tolerant opinion. . . .

At the start of Shakespeare's play, therefore, when Othello's role in the state is clearly shaped by the pressure of external foes and while his transgressive marriage is subsumed by matters of state, the play appears to challenge every aspect of the traditional depiction of black characters on the stage and in early modern culture. Othello himself is neither hungry for power for himself, nor portrayed as sexually voracious. But it is part of *Othello*'s continuing power to disturb us that, as events unfold, it may be that the stereotype, apparently bucked at the outset, "turns out to have a terrible and enduring hold on Othello's power to act. . . .

Othello's Descent into Rage

Numerous critics have understood Othello's descent into an incoherent rage, marked by the degeneration of his speech into the exotic lubricity of 'goats and monkeys' (4.1.265), as a reversion to some kind of buried savagery. The speed of his conversion to Iago's poison, his public renunciation of his wife, and the peculiarly ritualistic, even incantatory way in which he kills Desdemona—all have seemed to contribute to a racially determined characterization. . . .

Jack D'Amico discusses the play as a tragedy in which

> a man is brought to see himself as he believes others, including his wife, see him. What he sees is 'the Moor', the type set within the social perspectives of Venice. And, tragically, his inability to see himself as anything other than that Moor becomes a kind of proof that the negative image is not a mere illusion, and that what we had taken to be the noble man was, perhaps, something we as spectators imagined, as Desdemona imagined a certain man when she heard him tell his life story

This account suggests uncomfortably that we have been duped into suspending our knowledge of the operative stereotype: we allowed ourselves to forget the inevitable consequences of Othello's blackness. In all these critical cases some uncontrollable passion constructed as racially and racistly intrinsic recurs when Othello is plunged into jealousy and into an atavistic, uncivilized viciousness. . . .

Othello as an Outsider

Another way of interpreting the connection between Othello's jealousy and his race is to see it as the contextual property of the outsider. Thus Othello is made jealous by an Iago who preys on his weakness, his feelings of insecurity as a foreigner marked out in a sophisticated and urbane city state such as Venice. Othello's jealousy is thus part of the fact that he is black, but not because this is biologically determined but because it is culturally determined. As Paul Robeson glossed it, 'it is because he is an alien among white people that his mind works as quickly, for he feels dishonour more deeply', giving the play psychological accuracy as the depiction of the life of an outsider.

Race in the Criticism and Production of *Othello*

John Salway

John Salway was a British actor, director, writer, and teacher.

Salway examines issues of race in Othello, *primarily as they emerge in the classroom, in criticism, and in theatrical production history. The long-standing conviction that civilization rests only in European culture has caused many readers to regard race as a distraction in* Othello. *In teaching the play, the racism of the students emerges as they laugh at Iago's insults. In the nineteenth century, the casting of a black actor, Ira Aldridge, in the role of Othello (instead of a white actor in blackface) caused public outrage, and Edmund Kean, a white actor, eschewed the usual blackface to make Othello tawny skinned. Although some twentieth-century critics have overlooked or denied that race is an issue in the play, Salway quotes lines that reveal that racial prejudice was widespread in Venice and that race is indisputably central to the play. To realistically confront the subject of race in* Othello, *the lead, writes Salway, must be played by a black actor.*

The concept 'civilization' is conventionally used in ignorance of the racism which has shaped it. This key idea of Western culture was most popularly developed, perhaps, by Kenneth Clark in his TV series. He comments on the difference as he saw it between the Belvedere head of Apollo and an African mask belonging to Roger Fry:

John Salway, "Veritable Negroes and Circumcised Dogs: Racial Disturbances in Shakespeare," in *Shakespeare in the Changing Curriculum*, edited by Lesley Aers and Nigel Wheale, Hampshire, UK: Taylor & Francis Books Ltd., 1991, pp. 108–124. Copyright © 1991 by Taylor & Francis Books Ltd. All rights reserved. Reproduced by permission.

Whatever its merits as a work of art; I don't think there is any doubt that the Apollo embodies a higher state of civilisation than the mask. They both represent spirits, messengers from another world—that is to say, from the world of our own imagining. To the Negro imagination, it is a world of fear and darkness, ready to inflict horrible punishments for the smallest infringement of a taboo. To the Hellenistic imagination it is a world of light and confidence, in which the gods are like ourselves, only more beautiful, and descend to earth to teach men reason and the laws of harmony.

He seems unaware of the great Benin or Ethiopian civilizations. Neither does he consider the ironic possibility that an African craftsman produced this piece of 'authentic culture' sensitive to the demands from Western tourists at a time when 'civilized' Europeans were violently converting the continent to Christianity. Change places and, handy-dandy, who is civilized and who the barbarian?

It is the centrality for the European outlook of this orientalist concept of the Negro, the Turk, and the Asian which makes *Othello* such a significant text. It has always deeply troubled English genteel taste, especially in the way its eponymous hero is represented in the theatre. Here, at the heart of a white world, in the very bosom of European civilization, is a Black man. Few scholars, actors, critics, and directors, though, have gone quite as far as Miss Preston of Maryland:

> In studying the play of *Othello*, I have always imagined its hero a white man. It is true the dramatist paints him black, but this shade does not suit the man ... Shakespeare was too correct a delineator of human nature to have coloured Othello black if he had personally acquainted himself with the idiosyncracies of the African race.

To be fair to Miss Preston, this is only a rather extreme instance of the whole tendency within English thinking to see

Othello's colour as a distraction from the play's real issues, a view rather surprisingly endorsed by no less a figure than C.L.R. James. This goes very deep. Coleridge's now commonplace remark about Iago's action as 'the motive-hunting of a motiveless malignity' ignores the fact that now stares us in the face: Iago is patently driven by a deep racist antipathy. There are thirteen racist references to Othello in the opening scene. But, it wasn't until Gamini Salgado's New Swan Advanced edition in 1976 that the cultural meaning of Othello's racial background and inheritance was seriously considered as a central issue in understanding the whole play, something that acutely problematizes the dramatic action, its contemporary significance for Elizabethan audiences and the history of its interpretation.

During a Theatre-in-Education programme on the play, thirty-four sixth-formers worked with me on Othello's speech to the Venetian senate in answer to Brabantio's accusation that he had corrupted Desdemona with spells and medicines. . . .

Preparations for this included careful attention to everything said about Othello in the first two scenes. I also fed in information about the cosmopolitan nature of seventeenth-century Venice. I didn't, though, mention 'racism'. But . . . questions about racial identity are to the point. The students . . . found it more difficult to imagine that Othello could be a highly distinguished and influential military leader in a European state than that he could be married to a white woman, even given that she was an aristocrat. But I think that the Elizabethans perceived this dichotomy between public and private roles in quite the contrary way. Brabantio, in particular, seems to see the political threat issuing from the bedroom rather than the boardroom.

With a third group I planned an initial session which did focus on the question of racism. I compiled a collage of utterances from the play, spoken by Iago, Roderigo, Brabantio, the Duke, and Desdemona which draw attention in various ways

to Othello's cultural identity. These were pictorially reproduced on a poster-sized sheet as a swirl of language fragments
round a blank centre. I asked the group, in pairs, to try to
sketch the character being referred to here. I then filled the
centre with some utterances of Othello himself and asked the
pairs to amend and expand their 'image'. We had worked with
these fragments in the drama studio earlier in the morning.
Each student had had a single utterance. Have conversations
with your pieces of language, I had told them. Meet each
other spontaneously. Developing this phase of practical drama
work. I framed the 'free exchange' with a number of speech
contexts; tell each other a joke; exchange coded messages; raise
the alarm at midnight; insult each other so no one else can
tell; accuse each other as if in court. Finally, each student had
to 'run the gauntlet' of the language with their eyes closed.
The fragments weren't shouted but whispered. My objective
was to make the racist implications fully visible and audible. It
isn't too difficult to slide into a lazy acceptance of the
'normality' of certain utterances, even to enjoy them.

Given Iago's position in the play in relation to the audience, this process of 'normalization' can be dangerously facili-
tated—as I discovered myself when I acted Iago in a fifth-year
secondary classroom some time ago. My Iago was a bright
spark, a cockney. . . . As soon as I opened my mouth, four
lads who had theatrically sat behind the half-circle of the
'audience' grinned and nudged each other. When I bellowed
up to an imaginary Brabantio that an old black ram was tupping his white ewe, they exploded into paroxysms of stifled
giggling. One of them had suggested in a small group
'discussion' I overheard earlier in the lesson that Othello ought
to return to the rainforest. The four had then broken into a
spontaneous chorus of 'Jungle Bells'. Rarely does *Othello* con-
nect with such demotic [folkish] political energies in the professional theatre. I discovered a great deal about Iago from
that particular audience. . . .

Comparing *The Tempest* with *Othello* suggests some interesting parallels. As Caliban is lodged in Prospero's own cell, so Othello is admitted into the very bosom of European culture. Here, too, the privileged alien is seen getting uppity and trying to seduce a white girl. In both cases, the girl's father sees this as a violation of honour.

Curiously enough, a very similar view is taken by Samuel Coleridge and the *Athenaeum* theatre reviewer in response to the performance of the Black actor Ira Aldridge in *Othello* at the Theatre Royal, Covent Garden, opposite a white actress. They had been used to Othello being played by a blacked-up white actor. Ruth Cowhig reminds us that Edmund Kean had 'made the part of Othello his own' and established the convention of presenting the character as a 'tawny moor'. Ira Alridge's sudden appearance as a 'blackamoor' was evidently a rude shock to tender English sensibilities: 'it would be something monstrous to conceive the beautiful Venetian girl falling in love with a veritable negro'. . . . Samuel Coleridge was even more vehement: 'we protest against an interesting actress and a lady-like girl, like Miss Ellen Tree, being subjected by the manager of the theatre to the indignity of being pawed about by Mr. Henry Wallack's black servant.' . . . It's difficult now to grasp fully the radical significance of Shakespeare's characterization of Othello or the thoroughly disturbing impression that the original production must have had on its audience, albeit that the part would have been played by a blacked-up Burbage or Swanston [actors in Shakespeare's troupe]. . . . Othello, though, seems culturally assimilated into white society, a Christian convert, a man of nobility. He is also the indispensable military leader whose job is to defend the Venetian state against the threat of another barbarous 'other', The Turk. Black is pitted against Black. . . .

None of the characters in *Othello* have any problems with the idea of Othello as a distinguished soldier to be honoured as a guest in that particular role. The problems begin when he assumes a new and unexpected role—that of Desdemona's husband. Such a possibility is inconceivable to the patrician culture of Venice. Perhaps it is the very implicit prohibition on intimate relations between Black foreign soldiers and white aristocratic ladies that, paradoxically, permits the relationship between Desdemona and Othello to develop in the first place. They have to improvise, to make up rules of engagement as they go along. That the anxieties of the white, ruling elite extend beyond the question of their daughters' marriageability is made clear by Brabantio, who, told that the Duke is in midnight conference, resolves to take his grievance to his 'brothers of the state', thinking they will certainly be sympathetic to his view:

> For if such actions may have passage free,
>
> Bondslaves and pagans shall our statesmen be.
>
> (I.2.98–9)

What concerns Brabantio here are the possible consequences of Othello's marriage with Desdemona. He sees it as an implicit subversion of the whole Venetian social order.

Critical comments like those of Kenneth Muir, 'It is significant that only Iago and Brabantio seem to have any colour prejudice against Othello', alert us to the need to engage our students in a process of active reading which considers the complexity of racism as an ideological force. Apart from the fact that Kenneth Muir has overlooked Roderigo's reference to Othello as the 'thick-lips', we should see 'colour prejudice' as not just a question of the conscious, overtly racist utterances of a Iago ..., but far more as a matter of those unconscious utterances, unrecognized symptoms of an underlying culture of racism which propagates extreme racist attitudes and behaviour. The fact that traditional literary analysis of the play has avoided it and pursued such absurd irrelevances as whether or not Othello is truly noble or merely self-dramatizing is itself a sign that the culture of racism has been at work in the very heart of liberal humanism.

In my experience, the most intense debate focuses on utterances such as the Duke of Venice's throwaway comment to Brabantio:

> If virtue no delighted beauty lack
>
> Your son-in-law is far more fair than black.
>
> (I.3.286–7)

and Desdemona's apparently innocent remark:

> I saw Othello's visage in his mind.
>
> (I.3.249)

and there are particularly significant discussions to be had on such questions as how far Othello himself, as represented in Shakespeare's text, is self-oppressed, a victim of what [reggae icon] Bob Marley calls 'mental slavery'. Key textual moments here are:

> ... Her name that was as fresh
>
> As Dian's visage is now begrimed and black
>
> As mine own face.
>
> (III.3.383–5)

or:

> ... one whose hand
>
> Like the base Indian threw a pearl away
>
> Richer than all his tribe.
>
> (V.2.342–4)

or:

> ... in Aleppo once
>
> Where a malignant and a turbaned Turk

Beat a Venetian and traduced the state,

I took by the throat the circumcised dog

And smote him thus.

(V.2.348–52)

Although there is considerable textual evidence to suggest that Othello has come to think like a Venetian about all those who are not Venetian, we can't ignore what indicates, on the contrary, that his own history and cultural identity are still strong within him. . . .

The vast majority of white male critics seem to have shared both Brabantio's and Samuel Coleridge's (not to mention Iago's) disbelief that a 'lady-like' white girl could possibly find a 'veritable negro' sexually attractive. But, then again, there is in the play the contrary notion of the Black as 'lusty', as 'an old black ram', as possessing a sexuality highly dangerous to the secure nightcaps of white husbands, a paranoid complex most evident in Iago's salacious imagination. There is an irreconcilable duality in white ideas about Othello's attractiveness. He might have 'declined into the vale of years' but he is still an 'erring barbarian of here and everywhere', quite capable of 'making the beast with two backs', a figure of orientalist fantasy.

Othello has frequently been treated as a magnificent, atypical aberration, a kind of special racial case. . . . References are made to barbaric superstition in apparent innocence of the fact that even renaissance Christendom was riddled with it. The problem of the white representation of a Black person is . . . one that affects both literary criticism and theatrical production. It is a question of the invisibility to white eyes of Black people as agents of their own cultures and histories. What the theatre reviewers of 1833 were, in effect, denying to Ira Aldridge was his capacity to represent a Black character in white theatre. That, it was implicitly argued, could only be adequately done by a white actor. Ira Aldridge, the foreign, negro actor stepping into the all-white world of the Theatre Royal, Covent Garden and daring to touch, even symbolically, the body of Ellen Tree, was actually mirroring in social reality the predicament of Othello in the dramatic fiction being portrayed. . . .

But the far-reaching implications of Shakespeare's *Othello* cannot be unfolded unless the play, in reading and performance, is thoroughly informed by a Black presence in the role of Othello and charged with the experience of Black histories and cultures which throw important new light on areas of the text previously obscured or misunderstood. It is in that sense that we whites (that is, most of us reading this book) are very much the problem when it comes to an adequate overstanding of *Othello*.

Contemporary Perspectives on Race

A Backlash Has Occurred Against President Obama's Race

Dan Kennedy

Dan Kennedy is an assistant professor of journalism at Northeastern University in Boston.

In the following essay, Kennedy asserts that the election of the first African American president of the United States has unleashed an ugly and hateful racism in white American culture. The drama began before Obama had had a chance to propose any policy, he says. Immediately it became apparent that anything the black president did or proposed would be attacked. Elements within the population began spreading the rumor that Obama was a Muslim, a lie that many Americans accepted without question. Kennedy is convinced that racism in American politics is going to get worse before it gets better.

The August [2010] madness into which America has descended is about several things. It's about the still-sputtering economy, of course, and the fear it engenders. It's about xenophobia, never far below the surface. And it's about a rightwing media-political complex that plays on the public's ignorance.

But there's a unifying theme that few wish to acknowledge. What we are witnessing at the moment is the full, ugly furore of white backlash, aimed directly and indirectly at our first black president.

Racism Arises with Election of Black President

The case was made, inadvertently, in a *Wall Street Journal* op-ed piece [in August 2010] by Republican congressman-turned-lobbyist Dick Armey, the godfather of what might be called the Tea Party movement's corporate wing. Armey and his co-author, Matt Kibbe, proudly dated the birth of the Tea Party to 9 February 2009.

Barack Obama's $800m stimulus bill was not approved until three days later. Which is my point. The most notorious political movement of the Obama era, grounded in racial fears if not flat-out racism, sprung into being within weeks of Obama's inauguration, before he'd had a chance to do anything, really. If Obama was for it, they were against it.

The Tea Party winter and spring of 2009 led to the "death panels" of summer, and to rightwing hero [radio and television host] Glenn Beck's declaration that the president harboured "a deep-seated hatred for white people or the white culture". Minor issues involving Acorn, a heretofore obscure agency that helped register urban, mostly minority voters, became a cause célèbre. A little-known African American bureaucrat, Van Jones, was hounded out of office for having allegedly expressed offensive views about the terrorist attacks of 11 September 2001—views he later said he had never voiced and did not hold. Protesters spat upon and directed racial epithets at African American congressmen as the healthcare debate reached its climax.

Spreading a Lie That Obama Is Muslim

And now we come to the full fruition of all this race-baiting. According to the Pew Research Center for the People and the Press, 18% of Americans—and 34% of conservative Republicans—believe Obama is a Muslim, proportions that have actually risen since the 2008 campaign. Another poll, by CNN/

Opinion Research, finds that 41% of Republicans believe Obama was definitely or probably not born in the United States.

Far worse is the racial, ethnic, and religious hatred that has been unleashed, starting with the proposed Islamic centre to be built in New York several blocks from the devastated World Trade Centre site, which Obama endorsed and then (to his discredit) unendorsed, sort of, the next day.

Yes, we've all heard [conservative Republican former Speaker of the House] Newt Gingrich draw an analogy between Muslims and Nazis, and we all know that more than 60% of the public has expressed its opposition to what is inevitably, and inaccurately, referred to as the "Ground Zero mosque".

Other Racial Incidents in 2008 Campaign

But to experience the pure fury, you have to watch this video of a black man who had the temerity to walk through a group of people protesting the centre. It is a terrifying moment.

There is more—so much more.

—The anti-immigration law approved in Arizona, which made a star of Republican governor Jan Brewer, notwithstanding the inconvenient truth that illegal immigration across the Mexico-Arizona border is at its lowest level in years.

—The political crucifixion of Shirley Sherrod [who was forced to resign from a political post after parts of a speech were taken out of context and posted on a website].

—The continuing phenomenon of [former vice-presidential candidate] Sarah Palin, who, at long last, feels empowered enough to reach inside the deepest, darkest recesses of her tiny little heart and embrace a fellow rightwinger's repeated use of the N-word.

It's a frightening time to be an American and to watch this insanity unfolding all around us. There's a sense that anything could happen, none of it good.

A man stands in front of a billboard he sponsored in Wheat Ridge, Colorado, that questions the nationality and religion of President Barack Obama, November 21, 2009. Dan Kennedy argues that such demonstrations are part of a "white backlash, aimed directly and indirectly at our first black president." © John Moore/Getty Images.

Racist Media

What's all too easy to forget is that though Obama was elected with the strongest majority of any president in recent years, he received only 43% of the white vote. Now, it's true that no Democrat since Lyndon Johnson in 1964 has won a majority of whites. But it's also true that 100% of voters who would never support a black presidential candidate cast their ballots for someone other than Obama. Now they're roaming the countryside, egged on by the Republican party and the Tea Party and Fox News and [conservative talk-show host] Rush Limbaugh, looking for new objects on which to unload their bitterness.

The traditional media, built as they are on the notion of fair-minded coverage of equally responsible, equally reasonable political forces, can barely process what's going on. You literally cannot understand the current moment without watching the political satirists Jon Stewart and Stephen Colbert. But, hey, they're only comedians.

Anger and Racism Will Rise

Not that there's anything new about the Republican party's playing racial politics. Richard Nixon was elected in 1968 on the basis of his infamous "southern strategy", designed to appeal to white voters alienated by the historic civil-rights legislation shepherded through Congress by Lyndon Johnson. Ronald Reagan kicked off his 1980 campaign against the incumbent president, Jimmy Carter, in Philadelphia, Mississippi, where three civil-rights workers had been murdered, by invoking the toxic phrase "states' rights".

As the economy slides into another trough, with no prospect of another stimulus passing political muster, it's only going to get worse.

Strangely, there are virtually no political observers who hold out the prospect that the folks whom the right has alienated will turn out to vote against the Republicans this November [2010]. George W. Bush, after all, worked mightily to appeal to Latino voters. That's gone. Bush even won 70% of the Muslim vote in 2000. That's long gone.

The Republicans hope to ride the white backlash back to power, and perhaps they will. But they may also find that the hatred they have embraced will come back to haunt them this November—and well beyond. For the rest of us, though, the consequences of that hatred have yet to play out.

Miscegenation in Presidential Politics

Stephen Ducat

Stephen Ducat is a political reporter for the Huffington Post.

In the following selection, Ducat discusses comments made during the 2008 presidential campaign by anti-Obama citizens that mention the biblical injunctions against racial mixing. They hark back to America's racist past, when it was argued that racial mixing contaminated the white partner and lifted up the black one, and when a person was legally classified as black if he or she had a single drop of black blood. Ducat says public segregation may be illegal, but it still exists in private lives. He claims that at a deep level many, including blacks, believe that whites are intellectually and morally superior, because it is so embedded in our culture. He advocates for mindfulness of these attitudes in an effort to move beyond mere "tolerance."

The frank comments of unapologetic anti-Obama racists across the country have recently [in October 2008] gained a wide national audience. As Ricky Thompson, a pipe fitter from Mobile, Alabama, told a *New York Times* reporter, "He's neither-nor. He's other. It's in the Bible. Come as one. Don't create other breeds." Another denizen of the GOP's [Republican Party's] "real America" shared his spiritual insights with the same interviewer. Glenn Reynolds, of Martinsville, Virginia, pointed out, "God taught the children of Israel not to intermarry." Such shameless declarations of prejudice reveal something obvious but easily overlooked: It is not Obama's blackness that disturbs these pious bigots, but his grayness.

The Miscegenation of Obama's Parents

Ideas that now seem like crackpot notions of race were, not long ago, regarded as common sense, and found themselves codified in law. The "one-drop rule" asserted that a single drop of black blood in an otherwise white citizen rendered that person black. Blackness was widely viewed as a contaminant that sullied white purity. (In antebellum America, white slave owners got around this problem by either denying the ordinary practice of raping and impregnating black women, or by justifying this predation as a racial improvement of the population of black slaves.) The rule was adopted by numerous state legislators in the first third of the 20th century, and used as the basis for Jim Crow laws [laws enacted between 1876 and 1965 which mandated racial segregation].

In 1924 Dr. Walter Plecker, a public health advocate who worked for Virginia's Vital Statistics Department, said, "Two races as materially divergent as the White and Negro, in morals, mental powers, and cultural fitness, cannot live in close contact without injury to the higher." It wasn't until 1967 that the U.S. Supreme Court proclaimed Plecker's *Virginia Racial Integrity Act* and the one-drop rule unconstitutional. This decision, which eliminated the ban on interracial marriage, bore the wonderfully apt title of *Loving v. Virginia*.

Sadly but not surprisingly, such legal victories have not kept Plecker's sentiments from being embraced by contemporary guardians of racial boundaries. And, Barack Obama, the child of a black African father and a white American mother, is for these folks the very embodiment of what must not be brought together.

As psychoanalyst Adam Phillips has succinctly observed, "We hold ourselves together by keeping things apart." While legally sanctioned racial segregation in public life may be moldering in history's dustbin, a corresponding segregation in our inner lives continues to structure our thoughts and emotions.

Categories of Good (White)
and Bad (Black)

Some people consciously, most unconsciously, hold on for dear life to the pure and invariant categories of "good" and "bad." Keeping them apart and unambiguously distinct helps us retain a reassuring infantile fantasy of safety, order and certainty. "Race" lends itself well to this process of splitting. Imagined as fundamentally unlike us, the racialized other becomes the perfect receptacle into which we are free to project all the wishes, impulses, and longings that we cannot bear to see in our ethnic group or ourselves. In other words, racism allows us to be all-good because there is someplace outside of us to put the bad.

Of course, this ruse we perpetrate on ourselves only works if we can sustain the delusion of absolute difference. Those who are more consciously racist rely on what [developmental psychologist] Erik Erikson called "pseudo-speciation," viewing other racial groups as separate species. "Inter-breeding" thereby becomes a psychological, as well as a theological abomination.

Speaking of spiritual matters, we should not be too surprised that most *openly* racist people are religious fundamentalists. This is not just because so many Biblical fairy tales endorse slavery, ethnic warfare and genocide, and inveigh against "race mixing," but because the structure of fundamentalist theology and racism are the same—they both rely on splitting. A recent example of this symmetry is the fundamentalist Christian Bob Jones University, which didn't overturn its ban on interracial dating until 2000. (This was done with considerable reluctance, and primarily to save George W. Bush from political embarrassment after having given a campaign stump speech in their chapel.) Such racist thumpers of holy books literally as well as metaphorically think in black and white terms.

Thus, the very visibility of Barack Obama—let alone his candidacy for the most powerful and, before Bush, the most esteemed job in the world—creates a category crisis of epic proportions. He not only mouths a rhetoric of transcending division, but is himself a seamless genetic integration of what should be immiscible. The decent, God-fearing racist must be plagued by unanswerable questions: What is this incomprehensible hybrid of badness and goodness? How can the same person contain that with which I identify and which I despise? What does that make me?

In the course of the [2008] presidential campaign, we have heard Republican ads and seen GOP viral emails that pose more rational-seeming derivatives of these questions: Who is Barack Obama? Do we actually know him? Doesn't he sound kind of uppity and elitist? Is he a Christian or a Muslim? Is he really like us? Didn't he grow up in one of those anti-American parts of America, like Hawaii?

Both Blacks and Whites Harbor Bias Against Blacks

By way of concluding, I want to emphasize that most Americans are not consciously racist, and would abhor the prejudice and ignorance manifested by the good white Christians cited above. But as Drew Westen and other researchers have shown, the majority of people—black as well as white—harbor an unconscious negative bias against anyone perceived as black. At a deep level, most of us make use of racial categories to navigate the world, manage its vague and unseen threats, and define our worth.

And why should we expect otherwise? Every person in this country is embedded in a culture and history founded on racist beliefs, practices, and emotions. There is no place to stand outside this psychological and social reality. It saturates our national sense of self and structures our neural networks.

What is possible, however, is to acknowledge and remain mindful of this ugly and disturbing legacy so that we can minimize its influence on how we treat others, and how we elect leaders to public office. And, as the enthusiastic throngs of citizens, here and abroad, attest, it is even possible to move beyond "tolerance"—to embrace and celebrate the fluidity of categories, cultures, and identities that Obama's candidacy has come to symbolize.

Stifled by Sound Bites

Ellis Cose

Ellis Cose is a contributing editor and columnist for Newsweek, *a prolific author, and the former chairman of the editorial board of the* New York Daily News.

Shirley Sherrod, a US Department of Agriculture employee, gave a speech in the summer of 2010 in which she explained how her youthful anger against white people had been dispelled by great compassion for, and reconciliation with, poor white farmers who had historically been favored over black farmers. A right wing blog took parts of the speech out of context to make it appear that the speech was a black racist slur against whites. It was broadcast by the conservative press, and Sherrod was fired. Cose writes that it was yet another instance of injustice when ideology replaces journalistic integrity.

Taken on its merits and in context, it was a beautiful tale of redemption and reconciliation: a story of one woman's journey from anger to compassion. But in the end, it became something infinitely less lovely: a sign of the stupidity of soundbite culture, of the pitfalls of racial hypersensitivity, and, perhaps most sadly, of the difficulty—indeed, maybe even the impossibility—of having (in this society, at this moment) a truly honest public discourse about race.

The woman at the center of the storm, Shirley Sherrod, was an unsung Department of Agriculture [USDA] employee until a clip posted on a conservative Web site seemed to show her admitting bias against whites. Conservative talk-show hosts bayed for blood; Sherrod was forced to resign. (The matter was deemed so urgent that she was ordered to pull to the side of the road and compose the resignation letter on her BlackBerry.) Then, when the full-length video of her speech revealed that instead of discriminating against a white couple, she had gone out of her way to help save their farm, Sherrod was swamped with apologies, was offered a new job at the USDA, and received a seven-minute phone call from President [Barack] Obama.

The American public, meanwhile, was left to wonder what the moral of this tale really is. For starters, it's about the idiocy that can follow when ideology replaces journalistic integrity. Real journalists draw conclusions from facts. The ideologues who attacked Sherrod forced facts to fit their preconceived notions.

But this state of affairs in the U.S. media has broader and more insidious repercussions, as Charles Ogletree, one of Obama's professors at Harvard Law School, makes clear in a new book. *The Presumption of Guilt* is an exhaustive account of the events that led to the arrest of Harvard professor Henry Louis Gates, who initially was suspected of breaking into a home that turned out to be his. After Obama criticized the Cambridge, Mass., police for acting "stupidly," conservative talkers exploded in rage, accusing the president of being a racist himself. The ensuing controversy threatened to derail Obama's health-care package. The White House tamped it down with a silly "beer summit" between Gates and the arresting cop. What could have been an interesting discussion about police authority and race in America was reduced to a narrative about two men who might have been friends had they only shared a Bud Lite.

That incident demonstrated how difficult it is for this nation's first black president in particular to talk about race. With conservative pundits and activists predisposed to accuse him of catering to blacks, it seems better that Obama keep his mouth shut—and for members of his administration to

Shirley Sherrod, a former US Department of Agriculture official, on August 24, 2010. On July 19, 2010, Sherrod was forced to resign from her position after an out-of-context video surfaced that suggested she discriminated against white farmers. © AP Images/Manuel Balce Ceneta.

go out of their way to show they have zero tolerance for bias from any quarter, black or white.

Conservatives would be suspicious of any Democratic president. But Obama's race seems to complicate things— particularly among certain groups. A *New York Times*/CBS poll of Tea Party supporters found that 73 percent believed Obama did not "understand the needs and problems" of people like themselves; 75 percent thought he rejected "the values most Americans try to live by." And a majority thought "too much has been made" of problems facing blacks. "What is really bothering these people is a sense that their position in the society is threatened, that they are going to be worse off tomorrow than they are today," says Cesar Perales, president of LatinoJustice PRLDEF. That anxiety, he believes, is rooted not just in America's economic troubles but in its demographic transformation: "Large numbers of Latinos, particularly darker-skinned Latinos, [are] coming into the country . . .

[And] having a black president makes it worse because that is evidence to [many] Americans that their world has changed." Given such fears, any sympathy Obama shows toward minorities is likely to be widely misconstrued.

In the long run, I believe Obama's presidency will have a powerful and positive impact on race relations. The presence of a thoughtful, competent black man at the helm of the world's most powerful nation cannot help but change attitudes for the better. The irony is that in this area, as in no other, he is barred from using his eloquence. For him to speak honestly, in ways that really could contribute to intergroup understanding, means risking the wrath of the right. Despite his platinum tongue, Obama's most important contribution to race relations will almost certainly have to be in what he is, not in what he says.

Interracial Couples Still Face Discrimination

Caylor Ballinger

Caylor Ballinger is a reporter for the El Paso Times, *a Texas newspaper.*

In the following article, Ballinger reports that though some of the stigma related to interracial marriage has gone away, couples still face discrimination. Ballinger sites the experiences of several couples to demonstrate current attitudes in the United States. In addition, the author notes and discusses the increased rate of divorce among biracial couples.

It has been 46 years since the Civil Rights Act was signed. However, interracial couples today still face problems.

Still, after dating for a few years. Lap and Julia Sui married with their parents' blessing in 2004.

"My parents were fine with our marriage, but the only thing they were concerned about was getting a divorce since divorce rates are much higher here," Lap said. "Marriage in our village is very strong. Almost nobody ever gets divorced."

Discrimination toward their son and daughter in Texas was something the couple was warned about by friends in North Carolina.

"People warned me that my children may be treated differently here," Julia said. "I really did wonder if they would."

Some people act surprised when they realize these are his children, Lap said.

"One time I took my son to Wagner Park and a woman came up and asked how come he is really white," Lap said. "The way she said it was kind of strange, I thought."

"In general, the comments come from people when they look at our kids," Lap said. "Things like, is your wife from Vietnam, and they will ask a lot of questions. I guess they are surprised."

Different Races but Strong Common Religion

The couple said the people of Lubbock have been very nice to them, and the only comments were out of surprise about the children.

"To me I look at them and they just look like normal cute kids and I think why would they have any problems?" Julia said. "Really, I am not worried for them. There are a lot of hard things in life. We will teach them how to let things go." Lap Sui, an anthropology professor at Texas Tech, moved as a refugee in 1996 to the United States from Gia Lai Province Vietnam; he was part of the indigenous minority Jarai. While working as an interpreter in 2001 at a North Carolina refugee resettlement agency, he met his wife Julia.

"In my language we don't even have words like race or ethnicity," Lap said. "Here racism is a common word."

Julia Sui is originally from Pensacola, Fla. and is currently working on her master's in applied linguistics at [Texas] Tech.

"The color of someone's skin makes no difference," Lap said. "It doesn't matter if they are black, white or brown."

"Culturally it could be an issue for some couples," Lap said. "We shouldn't be afraid of people who come from a different culture, though."

There needs to be a willingness to learn about someone else's culture, Julia said.

The couple said despite their differences their common bond in religion has been the link they share.

"We come from different cultures, but since we are both Christian it helps a lot," Lap said. "That is the common culture for both of us."

Marriage could bring challenges for any relationship, but having common beliefs and faith in the Bible is a big help, Julia said.

"The Bible has a lot of guidelines for marriage," Julia said. "The Bible says to submit to one another, and that solves a lot of problems right there."

Attitudes Toward Biracial Marriages Improving

Larry Jones, director of missions at the International Christian Fellowship Lubbock, said race is not the main factor that it used to be for couples.

"People not accepting interracial couples in terms of religious reasoning was particularly true in the past, but I do not think that is the case anymore," Jones said. "My experience is seeing people seek others with likewise spiritual values."

After being a missionary in Germany in the '70s when the number of interracial couples was significant, Jones said, the United States is still about 20 years behind Europe in terms of accepting interracial couples.

"I think in order to change the acceptance of interracial couples, it will just take time," Jones said. "Time has a way of working things out."

While problems may still exist for interracial couples, Jones said, the acceptance of these couples is evolving along with the acceptance of interracial children.

"I think the future for children of interracial couples is brighter than it has ever been in the past," Jones said.

Christina Harris, Ph.D., an assistant professor of cultural anthropology at Tech, said her experience as a child of an interracial couple was not always so bright.

"I've experienced discrimination as a child of an interracial couple and that was a real eye opener," Harris said. "My mother is Asian and my dad is white."

When she lived in Michigan in elementary school, Harris said, she remembered a difficult time when the class was studying World War II.

"We were studying Pearl Harbor in the second grade," Harris said. "A kid pointed at me and said, 'You did that.' I just remember crying a lot about that. "In middle school her family had moved to Japan, where, Harris said, she received another dose of discrimination.

"In sixth grade my family was living in Japan," Harris said. "I remember some Japanese kids would shout 'foreigner' and throw rocks at my sister and me."

Unfortunately, racism still exists, Harris said. Although in her case she said it was not a struggle and overall life has been a very positive experience.

"In the U.S. people see me as looking Asian, but in Japan I didn't quite look Japanese," Harris said. "It's such a complicated thing, but that's the way people are. We have to categorize people."

Need to Foster Cultural Awareness

Harris said she thinks that classrooms should incorporate more awareness of other cultures.

"There should be more cross-culture programming to show how different some places are," Harris said. "Miscegenation laws were stopped in 1967. That was so recent, and there needs to be more awareness."

Miscegenation laws were laws made by the states prohibiting the marriage of a white and non-white person.

Cristina Brădătan, an assistant professor of sociology at Tech, said awareness and tolerance are the keys to bring about change.

"Before 1967 it was not even allowed to marry someone from a different racial group," Brădătan said. "So I definitely think we have evolved."

In the United States, people define one another based on race and ethnicity, Brădătan said. When people talk about interracial marriages they talk also about interethnic relationships.

Higher Rates of Divorce and Past Legal Barriers

"When people talk about a Hispanic and white person as interracial they are not really interracial, they are interethnic," Brădătan said.

There are studies that show the high rate of divorce in the United States, but apparently interracial couples have even higher rates of divorce, Brădătan said.

"Some people interpret this as being out of pressure or not being that much accepted," Brădătan said. "Even if the attitudes have changed here, there is still prejudice in some places about these relationships."

Jacki Fitzpatrick, an associate professor of human development and family studies at Tech and president of the International Association of Relationship Research [IARR], said for some couples the social stresses are what may cause them to break up or divorce.

The IARR is an organization of approximately 700 members from different fields around the world who study relationships, both romantic and friendly, with the goal of having a better understanding of relationships through research.

"Some interracial couples report that the stresses have strengthened them," Fitzpatrick said. "They will bond closer because they are enduring everything together and demonstrating a degree of commitment."

Social stresses in addition to typical couple stress can end up being a positive thing for some couples, Fitzpatrick said.

"The key climate for interracial couple change was opened in the late '60s from a Supreme Court ruling of *Loving vs. Virginia*," Fitzpatrick said.

A Virginia interracial couple, Perry and Mildred Loving, were sentenced in 1959 to a year in prison for violating the Racial Integrity Act. That act prohibited a marriage between a white and non-white. The Supreme Court overturned all miscegenation laws in 1967 shortly after hearing that case.

"It offered protection that the couples didn't have in the past," Fitzpatrick said. "This was a turning point for couples who were concerned about being together."

Interracial couples still report experiencing more social stress than other couples, Fitzpatrick said. This stress can be classified into two areas of marginalization.

"The first is passive marginalization, where people aren't necessarily hostile to them but may treat them as invisible," Fitzpatrick said.

An example of this would be an interracial couple who wanted to get a Valentine's card that looks like them, Fitzpatrick said. When they see all cards without any depiction of an interracial couple, it can make them feel invisible.

Marginalization

"The second kind is active marginalization, which is where people are going out of their way to make it difficult for the couple," Fitzpatrick said. "It could be someone unsolicited in a restaurant says an insulting remark."

In the last two decades there has been less active marginalization reported, Fitzpatrick said. However, passive marginalization has increased overall, so there are still a lot of stresses.

"Passive marginalization is very easy to see, but it is very hard to understand invisibility if you have never felt it," Fitzpatrick said.

Urban areas have reports of less marginalization, Fitzpatrick said. The argument is that larger cities have a more diverse population and tend to be more liberal or open-minded to interracial relationships.

"Explanation fatigue can also occur when interracial couples meet family and friends who may seem quite open to their relationship," Fitzpatrick said. "It may be that they are just curious, but it could be the hundredth time the couple is answering the questions and the social demands that keep happening over and over could take a toll."

Kayli Cross, a second year master's student in the Marriage and Family Therapy program at Tech, said that while working in the Tech family therapy program as the clinic coordinator the interracial couples she has worked with face the same issues that any other couple face.

"Sometimes the work towards finding compromise and common ground can be more challenging," Cross said. "I think it can definitely be done and these relationships can be, and are very successful."

Interracial relationships have finally become more of a norm than an exception, Cross said. This population is still in the minority, but it is more accepted now than it ever has been.

"From doing assessments here in our clinic," Cross said, "many people check more than one box for ethnicity or check biracial."

Luis Ramirez, a Ph.D. assistant professor of sociology at Tech, said one of the issues the census is dealing with is people who do not know which group to identify with.

"Cultural conflict, it's a catch between two cultures," Ramirez said. "Interracial couples face the question: how will their child be viewed by the family?" Recently in Louisiana a judge banned a marriage between a white woman and a black man because he said his concern was for the child, Ramirez said.

Judge Keith Bardwell, a Louisiana justice of the peace, refused to grant a marriage license to Beth Humphrey, a white woman, and Terrence McKay, a black man, in October of 2009. He defended the license denial by saying it was because of his concern was for the children, and he did not think society would accept the child. The couple was married by another justice and they are seeking legal action against Bardwell.

"My wife, who is Anglo, and I am Hispanic," Ramirez said. "We've never had any problems, and both of our parents were very accepting. Research does show that these experiences are not always so great."

Jeffrey Williams, a professor at Texas Tech and department chair for sociology, anthropology and social work, said he thinks couples in interracial relationships still face a lot of problems.

Influence of the History of Slavery

"I think issues facing interracial couples are incredibly prevalent today," Williams said. "Not talking about it doesn't help the situation."

The ethnocentric society is one that views itself as the best society and with the best practices, Williams said.

"Ethnocentricity gives us global diversity," Williams said, "but when you are trying to develop it can be difficult."

Williams said his daughter is white and she married a Hispanic man and the interracial aspect was a topic of conversation for some.

"It was not even mentioned in our family," Williams said. "However, the fact that she was white was discussed in his family."

The United States is not the only country to experience problems with interracial relationships, but the issues faced here are different from other countries, Williams said.

"One thing that makes us different is, our society has had a history of slavery," Williams said. "We abolished slavery and made an effort to incorporate those who suffered into society. A lot of other countries did not make that incorporating effort."

The United States still has a long way to go in terms of racism, Williams said. Part of the issue here was in the culmination of immigration, migration and forced entry into this country. This results in people who wouldn't normally be together.

"Race is a culturally constructed set of eyeglasses," Williams said. "Everyone has different lenses and so everyone sees things differently."

Adjusting to eating rice every day was a cultural change Julia Sui became aware of quickly when she married Lap.

"You need to be understanding to different values and cultures," Julia said. "Nobody's perfect, and people will do what they will. It helps me to make allowances for people."

Not growing up in the United States has made the cultural differences evident to Lap Sui as well.

"Of course she has her American culture and there are still so many thing we don't know about each other's culture," Lap said, "but we have made adjustments for each other over the years."

The cultural differences have been a strength for the couple as they said they learn from each other every day.

"There are a lot of similarities I've noticed between his culture and people I have met from other countries," Julia said. "Learning from them helps me to appreciate people from other cultures."

For Further Discussion

1. Discuss the historical events that may have had a bearing on *Othello*. See Ackroyd and Holden.

2. Discuss the various points of view regarding Othello's color. See Sanders, Skura, and Salway.

3. Discuss the differing opinions on stereotyping in *Othello*. See Loomba, Skura, and Smith.

4. Why is Othello considered to be a polluter by Iago and the Venetians? See Loomba, Bovilsky, Newman, and Adler.

5. What attitudes in 2009 and 2010 show the continuing racism in contemporary times? See Cose, Ducat, and Kennedy.

For Further Reading

Thomas Kyd, *The Spanish Tragedy*. c. 1584–1589.

Christopher Marlowe, *The Jew of Malta*. 1590.

————, *Tamburlaine the Great*. 1590.

Thomas Middleton and William Rowley, *The Changeling*. 1622.

William Shakespeare, *Antony and Cleopatra*. c. 1606–1607.

————, *The Merchant of Venice*. c. 1596–1598.

————, *A Midsummer Night's Dream*. c. 1594–1596.

————, *The Tempest*. c. 1610–1611.

————, *Titus Andronicus*. c. 1591.

John Webster, *The White Devil*. 1612.

Bibliography

Books

Jane Adamson   *"Othello" as Tragedy: Some Problems of Judgment and Feeling.* Cambridge: Cambridge University Press, 1980.

Marc Aronson   *Race: A History Beyond Black and White.* New York: Athenaeum, 2007.

Fredson Bowers   *Elizabethan Revenge Tragedy, 1587–1642.* Princeton, NJ: Princeton University Press, 1966.

Michael Brown   *Whitewashing Race: The Myth of a Color-Blind Society.* Berkeley and Los Angeles: University of California Press, 2003.

James L.   *The Properties of "Othello."* Amherst:
Calderwood   University of Massachusetts Press, 1989.

J. Kameron Carter   *Race: A Theological Account.* New York: Oxford University Press, 2008.

Celia Daileader   *Racism, Misogyny, and the "Othello" Myth.* Cambridge: Cambridge University Press, 2005.

Stephen   *Will in the World.* New York: Norton,
Greenblatt   2004.

Andrew Hadfield   *A Routledge Literary Sourcebook on William Shakespeare's "Othello."* London: Routledge, 2003.

E.A.J. Honigmann   *The Texts of "Othello" and Shakespearian Revision.* London: Routledge, 1996.

Stanley Edgar Hyman   *Iago: Some Approaches to the Illusion of His Motivation.* New York: Athenaeum, 1970.

Eldred Durosimi Jones   *Othello's Countrymen: The African in English Renaissance Drama.* London: Oxford University Press, 1965.

Julius Lester   *Let's Talk About Race.* New York: HarperCollins, 2005.

Virginia Mason   *Othello: A Contextual History.* Cambridge: Cambridge University Press, 1994.

Lois Potter   *"Othello." Shakespeare in Performance.* Manchester, UK: Manchester University Press, 2002.

Marvin Rosenberg   *The Masks of "Othello."* Berkeley: University of California Press, 1961.

Vincent Sarich and Frank Miete   *Race.* Boulder, CO: Westview Press, 2004.

Periodicals

Janet Adelman   "Iago's Alter Ego: Race as Projection in *Othello*," *Shakespeare Quarterly*, vol. 48, 1997.

James R. Andreas   "Rewriting Race Through Literature: Teaching Shakespeare's African Plays," *Shakespeare Yearbook*, vol. 12, 2001.

Kenneth J. Arrow   "What Has Economics to Say About Racial Discrimination?," *Journal of Economic Perspectives*, Spring 1998.

Emily Bartels   "Making More of the Moor: Aaron, Othello, and Renaissance Refashionings of Race," *Shakespeare Quarterly*, vol. 41, 1990.

Harry Berger   "Three's a Company: The Spectre of Contaminated Intimacy in *Othello*," *Shakespearean International Yearbook*, vol. 4, 2004.

Jonathan Crewe   "Out of the Matrix: Shakespeare and Race," *Criticism*, vol. 8, 1995.

Peter Erickson   "Representations of Blacks and Blackness in the Renaissance," *Criticism*, vol. 35, 1993.

K.W. Evans   "The Racial Factor in *Othello*," *Shakespeare Studies*, vol. 5, 1969.

Kim F. Hall   "Beauty and the Beast of Whiteness: Teaching Race and Gender," *Shakespeare Quarterly*, vol. 47, 1996.

Maurice Hunt   "Predestination and the Heresy of Merit in *Othello*," *Comparative Drama*, vol. 30, 1996.

Paul H.D. Kaplan   ""The Earliest Images of *Othello*," *Shakespeare Quarterly*, vol. 39, 1988.

Judson T. Landis   "Marriages of Mixed and Non-mixed Religions," *American Sociological Review*, June 1949.

Hope Laudrive and Elizabeth A. Klonoff	"Schedule of Racist Events," *Journal of Black Psychology*, November 2010.
Dave Lister	"Can It Be Wrong to 'Black Up' for Othello?," *Independent* (London), August 7, 1997.
Sharon O'Dair	"Teaching *Othello* in the Schoolhouse Door: History, Hollywood, Heroes," *Massachusetts Review*, vol. 41, 2000.
Martin Orkin	"*Othello* and the 'Plain Face' of Racism," *Shakespeare Quarterly*, vol. 38, 1987.
Hyman Rodman	"Technical Note on Two Roles of Mixed Marriages," *American Sociological Review*, October 1965.
Robert M. Sellers and J. Nicole Shelton	"The Role of Racial Identity in Perceived Racial Discrimination," *Journal of Personality and Social Psychology*, vol. 84, 2003.
Ian Smith	"Barbarian Errors: Performing Race in Early Modern England," *Shakespeare Quarterly*, vol. 49, 1998.
Shawn Ulsey, Joseph G. Ponterotto, Amy L. Roberts, and Anthony A. Canselli	"Racial Discrimination, Coping, Life Satisfaction and Self Esteem Among African Americans," *Journal of Counseling and Development*, Winter 2000.

Daniel Vitkus   "Turning Turk in *Othello*: The
Conversion and Damnation of the
Moor," *Shakespeare Quarterly*, vol. 18,
1996.

Index